THE ELEPHANT AND THE TWIG

THE ELEPHANT AND THE TWIG

The Art of Positive Thinking

14 Golden Rules for Success and Happiness

Geoff Thompson

CHIVERS

British Library Cataloguing in Publication Data available

This Large Print edition published by BBC Audiobooks Ltd, Bath, 2009.
Published by arrangement with Summersdale Publishers Ltd.

U.K. Hardcover ISBN 978 1 408 44176 3
U.K. Softcover ISBN 978 1 408 44177 0

Printed and bound in Great Britain by
CPI Antony Rowe, Chippenham and Eastbourne

All men dream; but not equally.
Those who dream by night
in the dusty recesses of their mind
wake in the day to find that it was vanity:
But the dreamers of the day are
dangerous men,
for they may act their dreams with eyes
wide open,
to make it possible.

T. E. Lawrence
The Seven Pillars of Wisdom

Contents

Foreword

by John Smyth

'But I'm a cartoonist, not a writer!' I bleated. At the end of the phone line I could feel rather than hear Geoff laughing to himself.

'You're articulate,' he said, 'you've written articles for magazines.'

I considered the brief scribblings that I'd put together for a rock music paper.

'But, but . . .' (I really did say 'But, but . . .' When I was a child I suffered with a very bad stammer. This had been largely cured by a sympathetic speech therapist, nevertheless sometimes in extremes it returns, and now seemed about the right time for it to do so again.) I was thinking, 'Why doesn't he get one of his heavyweight pals from the hallowed halls of academia to do the job? Surely nowadays, when you need someone to puff your book, you want someone with a bit of gravitas—a lettered professor, a judge, a captain of industry, a well-known retired gangster. Someone the public respects. Not a bloke that draws funny faces.'

*　　　*　　　*

And so . . . *The Elephant and the Twig.* This is a

1

book that needed a bold man as its author. The premise is simple: *'I, Geoff Thompson, am a very happy and successful person. You can be too.'* However well-intentioned and kindly meant, this sort of suggestion usually elicits a brief shocked silence followed by cries of outrage and horror. Who is this upstart who strides into the light of our campfire, beating his chest, proclaiming his success and happiness and frightening the horses? Those that have not yet recovered from surprise at the sheer vaunting cheek of the man, stare in silent amazement. Others, quicker to action, seek the sturdy branch of a nearby tree and a length of stout rope. How dare this man, infuriatingly optimistic and irredeemably bald as he is, dare to say that his life is full of joy? What self-deluding and outrageous fantasy is he pursuing? And . . . *'We can all be happy too!'* The man is obviously mad, a charlatan, a necromancer come to bind us with spells. There is, of course, the possibility that he is a well-known and retired gangster and that his claims to success and happiness are therefore quite genuine, but this is unlikely.

While the crowd leads Thompson, still smiling infuriatingly, toward the scaffold, let's for a moment consider his ravings. Let him meet his maker with his foolish optimism, his baseless belief in his fellow man and woman, and most particularly, his horrid and seemingly unassailable belief in HIMSELF as ashes in his mouth. Hearsay must not be allowed to flourish.

What are the facts? Admittedly we live in what the Chinese describe in an ancient curse as 'interesting times'. There is a malaise in society. Truth is, many people feel impotent, alienated, believing that their contribution to the world is, and ever shall be, as nothing. Like the poet Keats, they think their epitaph will read: 'Here lies one whose name is writ in water.' I think that Geoff would prefer the last words of Albert, the Prince Consort, who, upon breaking wind as he lay on his death bed, is said to have cried: 'As long as I can fart there's life in me yet!' Less poetic but certainly more optimistic.

We must concede the sad fact that legions feel trapped in dead-end jobs, unsatisfied, recriminating, bitter, quite literally wishing their lives away. Low self-esteem hides itself in racism, tribalism and general misanthropy. Few believe that any real contentment, let alone fulfillment, in their working lives is possible. How many people rise forlornly from their beds on a Monday morning dreading another week of the daily grind?

Geoff Thompson believes that people have the power within themselves to break free of the work that is killing their hopes and dreams, and that they can be the persons that they wish to be. Once imbued with determination and confidence, they can become artists, writers,

3

musicians, financial wizards, inventors, leaders of industry and nations. The reach of aspiration is limitless.

He also makes the case for satisfaction and real joy in humble but *committed* work that, although not especially financially rewarding, is of equal worth alongside the careers of the great and the good. Perhaps this work might be in caring for others or raising a family with love and wisdom. Even tasks, which to others might seem ostensibly mundane, can give to those that perform them with diligence and care, the deep satisfaction of a job well done.

The necromancer's 'secret' is that the ordinary man or woman can make themselves extraordinary—neither by genetics nor by any mysterious 'gift', neither by inheritance nor blind luck, but by an act of will. Central to Geoff's philosophy is that this power, this ability to recognise one's own potential is not itself a gift given by good fortune to a happy few, but is part of every person's make-up; part of everyone's birthright as surely as we are given a head, heart and eyes to see. Geoff's forte is in pointing out the ways in which this will to succeed can be nurtured and trained.

Despite considerable prowess in martial arts, in business and as a writer, Geoff unashamedly proclaims and indeed jealously defends his claim to be 'ordinary'. His contention is that success should be the natural lot of mankind. This is no false humility, as a brief anecdote will illustrate.

Geoff was engaged for a signing of his books at Foyles bookshop in London, possibly the most famous booksellers in the world. This was part of a major book-signing tour that Geoff and his wife, Sharon, had arranged right across the country. To promote the events, Geoff asked me to paint a seven-foot high advertising sign that would travel with him. On the morning of the important promotion at Foyles, I phoned Geoff. Crucified with embarrassment, I confessed that on the advertising sign that had been couriered up to the venue that morning, incorporating a huge smiling picture of him, I had made an elementary spelling mistake. In similar (happily few) circumstances I have had clients curse me to seven generations and wish that a murrain fall upon my flocks, so I made the phone call with some trepidation.

'Don't worry,' said Geoff, 'if there's a dumb spelling mistake on my sign it'll just make people more certain that I'm an ordinary bloke who makes cock-ups just the same as they do. In fact, I may get a few in just to have a laugh at me and that'll be fine too.'

Geoff talked at length to a spellbound audience. He stressed his belief that violence is only the option of the last resort. He spoke of the value of spirituality, morality and positivity. He appealed to his listeners to train body and mind in tandem and to take joy in

5

discovering the potential within themselves. His audience was receptive and enthusiastic and he sold a large number of books. Strangely enough, he spent a very substantial part of his time talking about other people's books, praising them and encouraging them to buy them instead of his own books. I turned to Sharon and said, 'He's flogging everyone else's books when he's supposed to be selling his own!'

She looked at me and smiled, 'He always does that,' she said.

Introduction

Have you ever heard the story of the Elephant and the Twig? In India they train obedience in young elephants, to stop them from escaping, by tying them to a huge, immovable object, like a tree, when they are still very young. The tree is so large that no matter how hard the baby elephant pulls and tugs it cannot break free. This develops what is known as 'learned helplessness' in the creature. After trying so hard and for so long to break the hold, only to be thwarted time and again, it eventually believes that, no matter what it does, it cannot escape. Ultimately, as a fully-grown adult weighing several tons, they can tie it to a twig and it won't escape, in fact it won't even try.

Often in life we're the very same; if told enough times that we cannot escape mediocrity, or that we cannot escape our environment, then eventually that belief will become so strong, so real, that we, like the elephant, will believe it; it will become our truth. Subsequently, due to our limiting belief system, we tend to think small. When I worked in a factory my life revolved around getting paid on a Friday; my thoughts were no bigger than that. Mondays were such a dread that often my weekends were spoiled in anticipation of having to go back to the oil, the

7

grime and the procrastination. This was my lot, though I always suspected there might be greener pastures, if I ever even thought about escaping I was held back by an invisible force-field, a huge immovable object, that seemed impossible to break through. It took me thirty years and many failed attempts to leave my nightmarish reality and live my dreams but when I finally did I realised that 'the immovable' was actually not immovable at all, it was just a twig and that I could break it whenever I wanted to. I escaped into the great and exciting unknown, away from bullying foremen and the shrill of spinning lathes, away from the life I never wanted to lead. On my journey from the factory to freedom I learned fourteen golden rules that have helped my success and happiness to grow beyond measure. I'd like to share them with you in this book.

I'm amazed actually that it took me so long to realise that I could break the twig, because in retrospect I can see it was something I always knew, it was a belief that had been looking for crystallisation for some time, but my own fears refused to allow it form. It's almost as though it had been waiting for the right moment to manifest. Whenever my dreams threatened to come true I pulled back in alarm; the unfulfilled desire suddenly seemed a lot more reassuring than the real thing.

Once I did break the twig I realised that this is our world, we can have whatever we want, we can be whoever we want and do whatever it is that our hearts desire. If we don't want to turn a lathe, sweep a floor, deliver the milk or press keys on a supermarket till we don't have to. We are where we are through choice. The moment we decide to choose better will be the last moment we turn a lathe, and the first moment we start doing whatever it is we want to do with our very short lives.

It is our thoughts that trap us—they make it so—but equally it is our thoughts that can set us free.

Catching crabs

I watched a documentary about how fishermen catch crabs (no! Not that kind). They use a mesh basket with a hole in the lid just big enough for the crabs to climb through. Once more than one crab has crawled into the basket, the fishermen take the lid off; many of these gentle creatures of the sea climb in, but none climb out. Eventually the basket fills to the brim with crustaceans yet, despite the fact that there is no lid to keep them there, they still don't escape. Every time one tries to exit the cage the others pull him back again.

I was amazed, aghast. It was the factory. It was the story of my life. Every time I'd ever tried to leave a bad job, to break away, my

9

peers would do the exact same thing, they'd pull me back; 'What do you want to leave for? This is a steady job, this is a good number this, it's safe.' Or, 'You don't want to do that (whatever my new idea was), there's no security in that.' One day, tired of the same old narrative I replied to one of the old-timers, 'But I hate it here.'

It was the factory

'You haven't even given it a chance!' he scolded, 'you've only been here five minutes (I'd been there six years), this is a good number, jobs like this don't grow on trees.'

10

'So how long have you been here then?' I asked, suitably reprimanded.

The old guy thought for a second and said, 'Oh, about thirty years.'

'And what do you think of it?'

'It's crap,' he said without hesitation, 'I hate the place.'

Similarly when I told people that I wanted to leave a steady job (that word again) at the chemical factory they went white, their faces looked like they'd been rolled in flour. 'But what will you do, what about the mortgage, what if it doesn't work out, what if . . .'

It only usually took a few 'what ifs' to get my bottom twitching, and after the fear injection she'd rub in the usual calming balm of, 'It's not that bad there, you'll be all right, give it a bit of time, your dad's not done bad out of the factory.'

I felt like a little crab at the bottom of a basket full of big fat crabs. My belief system was almost non-existent. In the end, I caught the very infectious *steady job* malarkey myself, it is very catching, and as soon as an aspiration found form in my mind it was clubbed to death by my own inner voice, 'Who are you kidding? Who do you think you are? What's wrong with the job you've already got? It's a steady number, it was good enough for your dad . . .' etc. I'd been pulled back so many times that in the end self-deprecation and disbelief became a part of my inner core and the moment an

11

entrepreneurial thought swam into my mind it was drowned out by the voice of my inner warders. Many times I picked up my pen in a fit of inspiration to write what I dreamed would be the next bestseller, only to be thwarted by a faulty internal dialogue that was stronger than my will to continue. The pen would be discarded and replaced by bicycle clips and a ride to the factory for a night shift that I absolutely abhorred. Even today, twenty years on, the very thought of that long ride still inspires a depression that makes me feel so grateful to have found a way out. I used to sit in the works canteen in the dead of night when everyone else was tucked up in bed and think, 'What can I do to get out of this nightmare?' I felt so trapped. I had a family, a mortgage, HP payments, three children and a cat to feed, so many things that seemed to glue me to a job I hated. And the longer I stayed, the more glue I attached. But I could never think of anything else I wanted to do other than write, I had allowed others, and myself, to convince me that writing was not a real option and that I was dreaming, so I resigned myself to following in family footsteps and settling for the oil and grime.

I did a fair bit of moaning about the job too, I hated the hours, the dirt, the foremen, and I told everyone who'd listen that if it wasn't for my wife I'd be off like a shot, I told them it was her fault that I was there because she wouldn't let me leave. Then one day, after my usual moan, she did something unprecedented, she told me to shut my moaning gob and get a job that I did like if I was so unhappy. She gave me her permission. Well, I nearly fell over I was so shocked. And that was when the realisation hit, the truth. She wasn't holding me back at all, it wasn't her fault that I was stuck in a nightmarish employ, neither was it the fault of the old-timers or my peers; the fault was entirely mine. I was there out of choice.

Blaming others for my predicament was my way of hiding from the fact that I was scared, I had a choice but was frightened to choose better. I realised at this point that I was looking in the mirror not at a hard-done-by twenty-something but at a frightened youth with a penchant for procrastination and blame—if I didn't want to stay in a job, if I really wanted to leave the factory, leave the city, or even leave the country for that matter, nothing, no one would be able to stop me. If I put my heart and soul into doing something, and believed it could be done, had a little faith in my own power, even mountains would tremble. I could do anything, be anything and go anywhere. This was my world, my incarnation, and the free will I had given over to my influences I snatched back and started my journey. And I had a great vehicle too, probably the best bit of kit I'd ever own—my own unique body.

Shortly after the realisation and the shock, I left a steady job of seven years, with no other job to go to and no idea of how I was going to make a living, and entered the real world, a world of opportunity and excitement; and I've never looked back. It was brilliant, exciting and scary, so much to do, so many places to go. I made a decision—I broke the twig.

Rule One

We're all dying so now is the time to act

I have some good news for you and some bad news—as the joke goes. The bad news—and I'm very sorry that I have to be the one to tell you (someone has to do it)—is that we are all dying! It's true, I've checked it out, in fact I've double and triple checked it, I've had it substantiated and, well, there's no easy way to say it, we are dying. It's something that I always kind of knew, but never really chose to think about too much. But the fact is, within the next seventy or eighty years—depending on how old we are and how long we last—we are all going to be either coffin dwellers or trampled ash in the 'Rose Garden' at some local cemetery. Scary! Strange thing is, when we are brown bread the same rule will apply to the next generation of people that read this book; they've only got seventy to eighty years left too. So Rule One in the fourteen golden rules for success and happiness is: *'We are all dying so now is the time to act.'*

The good news is that now we have acknowledged our own mortality, and accepted the fact that we could be brown bread tomorrow, we can really start to live. All those plans that you have on the back burner, you know, the great things that you are going to do with your life 'when the time is right' (the time is never *quite* right, I find) need to be brought forward and done now, this minute, pronto, in a hurry, as quick as your little legs will carry you. The novel that you want to write, the trip to the Grand Canyon you've always wanted to take, the vocational job you see in your mind's eye, the West End play you want to produce, you have to do them now. We're dying see! So putting them on the back burner until the circumstances are right means that they will probably never get done.

You owe it to yourself to go out and do them before it's too late. Tomorrow? It's all a lie, there isn't one, only a promissory note that we're often not in a position to cash. When you wake up for a new day, tomorrow will be gone and it'll be today again and all the same rules will apply. Tomorrow doesn't even exist. It is just another version of now, an empty field that isn't going to change unless we start planting some seeds. Your time, which is ticking away as we speak at about sixty seconds a minute, will be gone and you'll have nothing to show for it but regret and a rear-view mirror full of 'could haves', 'should haves' and 'would haves'. If you don't claim your place in the annals of history *now*, you'll end up as some sepia-coloured, unidentifiable relative, that no one can put a name to, in a yellowing photo album, which only gets a dusting down on high days and holidays. Your epitaph will read, 'Joe Smith . . . he didn't do much, did he?'

So what I'm thinking is (and this is not molecular science) if we are dying and the amount of time that we have left is just a few years or less, a tiny amount of time, almost insignificant if you start thinking about the millions of years that the planet has been spinning, if that's all we've got why the hell aren't we doing all the things that we want to do NOW?! What's all this 'back burner' malarkey? And why are we all waiting for the 'right time' when we already know that it isn't going to show? The 'right time' is the date that never arrives, the girl or boy that keeps you standing at the corner of the Co-op looking like a spanner. So, bearing all this in mind let's start filling up our baskets with the riches that life has to offer. When the Reaper comes a-calling we will have crammed so very much into our lifetime that the Great Auditor in the sky will recoil in disbelief and demand a re-count. You'll have achieved so much that you will be marked out in history as one of the few; someone who invested every second of their time, a shining example, and the template for future generations to model. Your CV will buckle table legs, people will read it and call you a liar because it will run for pages, and the Reaper will fall asleep waiting for your life to flash by because there'll be so very much.

Life is like a Pizza Hut salad bowl

Have you ever noticed when you go to Pizza Hut (great restaurant, one of my favourites) that they give you a rather small bowl and then say, 'Have as much salad as you can eat.' Life is like that small salad bowl, but like the hungry people waiting for their main course we can cram as much into that little bowl as we can carry. I love watching people go up to get their salad and stacking the food up like they're filling a skip. They stack slices of cucumber around the sides of the bowl to make it deeper then they fill it so high that they have to hire a forklift truck to get it back to the table. Fill your bowl, we come this way but once so let's make the very best of the short stay. Like the once a year holiday to Florida or Spain, fit as much into the short time as you can. Make sure that you go back knackered because you got so much done.

If you don't want to be a postman then don't be a postman, give it up and be a painter, a writer, a tobogganist, whatever, just don't be something that you blatantly are not.

And now is the time, not tomorrow. There is no time like the present. If you can't have what you want this very second then the very least you can do is to start the journey, now, this minute, while the inspiration is high. We all have the same number of hours in the day, it's just what we do with our time, how we invest it, that determines where our lives may lead.

Rule Two

You are your own god

I know that Rule Two might sound like sacrilege, and some may dislike me for even implying it, but: *You are your own god!* You are a co-creator with the universe, the man/woman that can make it all happen. Every religious text in the world will tell you the very same, that God is within, that the kingdom of Heaven is inside you and that, if you have faith in your own creative force you can make miracles happen. And it's true. But it's quite a weighty responsibility to take on, so most of us, giving in to our fears, balk at the task of taking control of our very own world. It is far easier to place our fate in the hands of others, or with the elements, and then blame anything and everything when things go awry than it is to take the wheel.

I think we all secretly know this and when the time is right, hopefully we will all take up the mantle with our intentions, make a hole in life so big that other, more timid souls may climb through and achieve also. You have the ability to change the whole world until it fits you like a Savile Row suit. If you are overweight you can become lighter, if you are underweight you can build yourself up, if you

19

are unhappy or unsuccessful or unfulfilled you have the power to change for the better. You can become the person you want to see when you look in the mirror, not an uninspiring reflection of someone you hardly know and perhaps don't even like. With faith you can move mountains. You can have anything and you can be anything, but for it to happen, you have to take responsibility for your world and *make* it happen.

You are a unique person, you are the only person in the world that looks through your eyes, hears through your ears, and speaks through your lips. Every time you touch something with your fingers you are the only person in the world, in fact, in the known universe, that actually feels what you touch. You are one in several billion. Every part of you is a one-off, an original, a masterpiece, the greatest bit of kit you'll ever own.

But as a species we don't use our gift to the full, it's like having a Formula One racing car sat in the garage that we never use because we are frightened of pulling out into the traffic, scared of scratching the paint work. We have a masterpiece in the attic, our potential, that we are unaware of and because we don't know it we cannot realise its benefits. We are the treasure at the end of the rainbow, we are the alchemist, pouring ingredients into a cauldron marked 'Life'.

We are the alchemists

You determine your world

Someone asked me once at a book signing what frightened me the most. Having worked as a nightclub bouncer for nine years facing woolly mammoths on a nightly basis, the questioner obviously thought I was going to tell of the nineteen-stone gypsy that wanted to bite my nose off, or the gang that placed a contract on my kneecaps. And for a moment I thought the same. These incidents did frighten me, but there was something that frightened me more. My own potential. When asked, I realised for the first time that my greatest fear, one that I dared not even acknowledge to myself until that moment, was my own potential. What I knew I could achieve with my life and what I knew I could become were more frightening than anything else imaginable, but at the same time the thought of my own potential was also exhilarating. What frightened me the most was the fact that now I had finally acknowledged my own potential I could no longer sit and do nothing about it. It would be a sin not to create, for myself and for the better good of others, now that I knew I was a creator. Abraham Maslow called it the 'Jonah Complex', the fear of success. He said that we are generally afraid to become that which we can glimpse in our most perfect moments, under the most perfect conditions, under conditions of greatest courage; we enjoy and even thrill to the god-like possibilities we see in ourselves at such peak moments and yet, simultaneously, shiver with weakness, awe and fear before the same possibilities.

That was me, frightened but at the same time excited about my own potential.

*We are generally afraid to become what
is possible*

I bumped into a guy at McDonald's the other
morning, we were both waiting for it to open,
him after just finishing a twelve-hour night-
shift working as a security man, me after my
early morning walk in the local park to start
my day. We started talking and within minutes
this chap—a nice man—got to telling me that
he worked for a local security firm, for very
poor money. He told me how he hated the job

and how, actually, he really wanted to be a professional singer; he was very good too (he said). I listened as he told his tale of woe about the security boss who never recognised his leadership qualities and why others always seemed to get promotion before him, and that, when he sang at the local karaoke he awed crowds, but just couldn't get a break because . . . 'Well, no one gives you a break these days do they?' When he'd finished, it took some time; there was a lot to complain about, I said, 'I think I know what your problem is, why you are not a singer, or at least why you are not on the way to being a singer.' The shop was just starting to open so we went inside ordered a coffee and continued.

'Why?' he asked, rubbing his sleep-filled eyes and ordering a Big Breakfast.

'Because you don't try hard enough,' I replied. My answer stopped him dead in his tracks. He was aghast; his mouth fell open like a cartoon cat. He looked at me as though I had just French-kissed his mother and he said,

'You don't even know me.'

'I don't need to know you,' I said, realising that I had probably said far too much already. 'If you are not there or at least on the way then you haven't tried enough. The only reason I know this,' I said honestly, 'is because I used to be just the same as you, happy to blame everyone but myself for the fact that I hated my lot.' I went on to explain—even though at this point I wasn't quite sure it was what he wanted to hear—that if he wanted to be a singer he should be spending twelve hours a night training to be a singer, instead of working for peanuts guarding empty industrial units. Why wasn't he hitting every open mike in the district, every night, to practise his art, writing to every record company every day until they got so fed up of his letters that they gave him a chance? Or studying his art, working his apprenticeship, making it happen. Why wasn't he meeting providence half-way down the street instead of waiting for it to knock at his door and then complaining because it didn't? Why, if all he wanted to do was be a singer wasn't he a singer? Probably because he just didn't want it enough. It's easier to sit on a bit of talent and blame the world for not recognising it than it is to go out to the world, develop that talent, face rejection, perhaps many times, and say, 'Listen, this is me, do you fancy a piece?'

This lad was one of the many that had a 'great idea', a seed, but who wasn't prepared to go out and do a bit of planting. He was one of the great majority who hated what he did but wouldn't do anything about it even though it was well within his power to do so.

I have a friend who is a top-turf accountant; he makes a lot of money from his work. He is brilliant, and judging from his opulent lifestyle his brilliance obviously pays very well. But he hates his job with an unrivalled passion. If he were to redirect his brilliance in another direction he would be 'brilliant' at anything he chose to do. Instead he prefers to fill his evenings with the same old 'I hate my job but I'm tied to it' complaint, that does just what it says on the packet—it ties him to a job that he hates. He'd tried a couple of times to change but had been knocked back. This was the basis of his gripe; that he wanted to move but others wouldn't give him a chance. It was their fault that he was stuck in a watching-paint-dry-profession that was turning him as grey as his pin-stripe. He completely disempowered himself when he projected the blame. If his predicament is *their* fault then his predicament will not change until *they* allow it, which most likely is never.

We must acknowledge that we are creators; a small piece of God, and the rest of the universe will conspire to help us achieve our aims.

Acknowledge and change or stop moaning about it

Colonel Sanders (Kentucky Fried Chicken) wanted to change a world dominated by steak restaurants into a world containing chicken-only restaurants. Over a thousand different companies told him that his idea, his dream, would not work and that he would never become the king of fowl. Many told him that his idea was naïve, some even laughed at the premise when he went to them for finance. Did he allow their lack of insight to kill his dreams; did he give up, hand over his power and blame others; did he lie down and die after yet another rejection letter and say 'maybe they're right'? No chance, they never even put a dent in the fender. He knew what he had, he believed in it emphatically, and if he believed in it, if he could see it he knew that there must be others out there who would believe in it and see it also. He just kept knocking on doors until he met that certain someone. He felt that each door he knocked on that gave a 'no' was one door closer to the one that would give a 'yes'. It took over a thousand rejections to get to that 'yes'. He finally got the backing he desired; now there is a Kentucky Fried Chicken restaurant in almost every city.

How many times have you been turned down? Not a thousand, I bet.

I will never give up, I refuse to quit because I know that no matter what others might say or do they cannot and will not deter me. The power is mine until I fall into the blame trap, then I give it over to the object of my blame. This I will never do, I refuse to. Colonel Sanders knew, as I know, that it was down to him and that no one could stop him unless he allowed them to.

I once received a fifteen-page letter from a man telling me in minute detail how bad he thought my writing was and that—in his opinion—it would never sell. He was absolutely insulted that I even thought myself worthy of becoming a professional writer. His letter was so scathing and so personal that it literally made me cry. I could have thrown the script in the bin and blamed this malicious and thoughtless man for my failure, I could have blamed a cruel world for not seeing my dream and for being so unnecessarily *personal*—and people would probably have understood. J. D. Salinger, who wrote the haunting classic *The Catcher in the Rye*, was so disturbed by one particular critique of his second book that he went into seclusion and never published another in his entire lifetime. The words of the critic crushed him. But by withdrawing from the world and depriving it of greater classics, Mr Salinger gave away all his power.

My critical antagonist could have done the same to me, but he didn't. I didn't allow it, I refused to be held back by anyone. His critique did not stop me from selling hundreds of thousands of books. It did not stop me from sending my plays to the top theatre in Britain and being taken onto their writers' group, neither did it stop me from selling my writing to some of the top magazines in the world and getting a job writing for a film company. On the contrary in fact, I would say that it has

28

actually helped me to succeed because it made me more determined than ever to carry on. It hasn't stopped me, and it never will; I am a lion and not a sheep. Every time I get a knock-back, a rebuttal or mud slung at me or my work, I think about Colonel Sanders and his thousand refusals and ask myself, 'How many times have you been knocked back? Has it been over a thousand times?' Of course it hasn't, so pick yourself up and carry on until someone says 'yes'.

Take responsibility for your own world and never project blame. If you do you lose your power.

Rule Three

You are what you think

Now that you have accepted Rule Two, your God-given right to create, and the responsibility that comes with it, you need quickly to learn Rule Three: *'You are what you think.'*

Most people in life fail to act because they fear the consequence of their actions; in fact they allow the fear of consequence to bully them into not acting at all. The consequence is rarely the problem in these cases, it is how we perceive the consequence. In other words, it's our thoughts that determine whether and how we deal with it. If we think 'I'll handle it' we most likely will, if however we think 'I couldn't handle it' then most probably we will not, in fact we will probably avoid making the decision that will bring about the consequence we are afraid of.

You must decide what it is that you want from life and how you are going to set about getting it. Of course, that's logical, but you also have to look at the consequence of having what you want and not be frightened off by it.

Creativity relies on faith in your own ability to create, but equally it relies on your ability to handle what you create. If part of you is

30

I can handle it!

frightened of the consequence, the failure or
success of creating, you are likely to sabotage
(consciously or unconsciously) your own plans
and subsequently create nothing. So when the
feared or revered consequence rears its head
and tries to intimidate, we must kill the
fledgling fear before it becomes a monster. We
do this with our positive thoughts because we
are what we think. We are unafraid and
optimistic because we think and encourage

31

positive thoughts and discourage thoughts of fear. We become afraid because we court and entertain negative thoughts and fail to encourage the positive.

What we focus on becomes our reality. If we focus on the good then every day is Christmas; if we focus on the bad every day is dark and no matter what material riches we have around us darkness will prevail. So focus on what you want, on how you want your life to be, choose only encouraging thoughts and starve to death anything that hints of fear—fear is the mind-killer. Choose the decor of your new world and then focus on it every day. From when you wake in the morning until you go to bed at night, tell yourself in your internal dialogue that you are the creator and that you can create—and handle—anything. Do this until it becomes a habit to think only positive thoughts.

We can only grow as big as our thoughts, we are defined by our thoughts, and we are the result of what we think about all day long. This is the truth so be very careful, what you think about is what you are likely to become. If driven and developed our thoughts can take us to the stars, but if left unattended they will drive us into the dirt. The choice is entirely ours. The great thing is, we do have a choice, if we practise religiously to make our thoughts great then it is inevitable that we will become great, it is only an idle and unattended mind that ends up sleeping in a bus shelter blaming life for its misfortune. It's not just a matter of reading it in a book and thinking about it for a day or so then moaning because nothing has happened, we have to work on it until thinking big, thinking positive becomes our habit, until negative and fearful thoughts do not even try to enter our minds. Those that do sneak past the sentry are plucked out, weed-like, before they have chance to seed. Initially this can be very difficult. Negative thoughts constantly try to invade your peace, but like anything else of worth, practice makes perfect. There is one thing in this magical universe that we have control over and that's our own thoughts, but we are so used to letting them and other people's thoughts invade and rape our consciousness that we often feel the opposite to be true. It often appears that we have no control whatsoever and the negative thoughts, like little electrical bullies in our grey matter, come and go at will. They squat in our heads, make a mess and then leave us in turmoil.

This is not an unsubstantiated hypothesis; at 39, nearly 40, my thoughts create a world that is idyllic, I love what I do, what I am and where my life is going. I have made my life this way by training my thoughts.

As a young man I was the opposite, and only because I allowed my thoughts free rein. Subsequently I was overrun by nagging and destructive thoughts that ate away at my mind until I was on the very edge of a nervous breakdown. On more than one occasion I felt that life was no longer worth living. One of the worst things for me as a depressive youth was my belief that I had no control over my own negative thoughts and that they could—and did—come and go as they pleased. I felt kitten-weak, I also thought I had to live under the dominion of bullying thoughts for the rest of my life. As far as I was concerned this was no life at all. Depressions seemed to swoop down on me at the most unexpected times and shatter my young life. I believed there was not a single thing I could do about it. My doctor offered his solution in a bottle of anti-depressants, my friends said I should *pull myself together*, my mum said I should *fight* it.

The tablets ended up in the river, my mates got a very wide berth because they made me feel like a weakling and my mother, bless her, guided me through with pep talks and solace until the depressions eventually lifted. Then one summer I had a revelation. The depression started on the first day of a two-week annual holiday to the seaside with my wife and children. I was devastated. It was back, uninvited, unwanted and, I believed, unstoppable.

At the first sign of depression the negative thoughts rushed into my mind; 'What if I get really depressed and spoil the holiday for my wife and children, I'll ruin everything, we'll probably have to go back early and everyone will say, "Why are you back early?" and we'll have to make up some excuse because I'm ashamed of being depressed.' The negatives rushed into my head and the downward spiral, the perpetuation, began. The more I looked at my lovely wife and kids the more I was sure I would spoil their holiday, and the more I thought, the more depressed I got. Just when all looked lost suddenly—from where I don't know—I found some courage. This very angry and indignant voice rose up from out of nowhere and boomed, 'That's enough, I'm not having any more of this, I will not spoil this holiday for my family, no matter what happens this holiday is going to be brilliant. I'm not having this any more. If I get depressed I'll handle it, I will deal with it, and I won't let the family know, this is going to be their holiday and I am not going to spoil it no matter how bad I feel. So do your worst, if you (the depression) want to come in then come in and let's get it on because I can handle it.' It was amazing. For the first time in my life I was fighting back. Then, as though by magic, the depression left as quickly as it had arrived. I discovered on that fateful holiday that I had a weapon to fight not only my own negative thoughts, but also the depressions. My mum always told me I should not 'give in to it' but I never actually knew how; now I did.

By fighting, by answering back, I could repel these negative demons. I could beat the fear of consequence by saying to myself, 'Damn the consequence, I can handle anything.' Even though every part of me wanted to run away, to hide from these feelings and thoughts, I stood my ground and not only challenged them but actually invited the feelings in, 'Come in,' I'd say, 'have a sit down, have a look around.' Then I'd sit with the feelings; I'd actually allow them—as nasty as they were—to wash over me. I wouldn't allow any thoughts to attach to them and I certainly wouldn't allow my fear to come out in words but I would sit in them, feel them, even question them, 'So what is this feeling?' I'd ask. 'What are you?' Then I'd tell the feelings what they were, what I knew they were; just big bundles of energy, and unless I latched onto them and panicked they couldn't hurt me at all. I'd imagine—as the feelings went through me—that they were ocean waves and I was riding on top, going with them, and not resisting at all. Then I'd say, 'Let's feel it again, I'd like to, please.' It might sound crazy but it worked, once I actually took notice of the feelings; once I invited them in they disappeared. It was amazing, once you face them down they lose their power, it is only when you cower and panic that they get any grip over you at all. It is difficult though because the feelings can be so overwhelming that you panic and think, 'Oh no, not again.' You have to practise overriding this normal reaction and attack as soon as the thoughts start coming and be pre-emptive with the feelings and invite them in. The thoughts need to be opposed or overridden, the feelings need to be welcomed and invited in. It sounds contradictory I know, but there is a method in my madness. Negative thoughts trigger negative feelings so you have to fight against them, oppose them, answer them back and talk over them so that they do not start, or perpetuate, negative feelings. If the negative feelings are already there then trying to resist them, panicking with them will only bring them on more. What we resist persists. So if the feelings come, accept them, invite them in, don't attach any thoughts like 'why am I feeling like this? Oh no, I don't like this' etc. If you do the perpetuation begins. Rather, if the feelings come, say to yourself, 'I like this, this is good, let's have a bit more, bring it on, I can deal with this all day long.'

If you don't fight the negative thoughts they will bring on the negative feelings, and if you don't accept negative feelings they will trigger negative thoughts, which in turn will trigger negative feelings—the downward spiral begins. It takes courage not to panic with these feelings. I know, I've spent a great deal of my life trying different techniques to control negative thoughts, fear of consequence, and often depression, and this is the only way I have found that works.

If you are looking at the future and the

negative thoughts rear their ugly heads, fight them from the start. If feelings of dread, or worse, come into your mind, invite them in and do not allow any negative thoughts to perpetuate them.

That's the only way to get rid of them; invite them in. These feelings are like blackmailers. Imagine if a blackmailer approached you and said, 'Give me some money or I'm going to send your partner these pictures of you snogging the photocopier at the work's Christmas party.'

If you turned around and said, 'Send them, I don't care,' you automatically take away all the blackmailer's power, he has nothing on you because you don't care what he does. Threats of consequence/depression are the same; if you panic when they blackmail, you give them your power and the more you panic the more power you give over. If, however, you say, 'Give it your best shot because I really don't care,' you take all your power back again.

An extreme example of the power of negative thought is the people who see the world as being a conspiratorial existence of darkness and doom. Their whole life is based upon the belief that walls have ears, the phones are bugged, there are encrypted messages in the barcodes at the supermarkets, that a malevolent force is constantly trying to rule the world and that this force is darker and stronger than any force for good and no matter what we do or say nothing can change it. They talk about this *passion* with such fervour that, during discussions, they come close to tears. These types, as you can imagine, are so infectious that you come away from every conversation feeling down for days. Whoever they talk to gets dragged into their world until they believe it too. They sit around for endless hours talking about the darkness of the world, trying to discover hidden truths. This is their world because they make it so with their thoughts. I choose different, I choose better.

My world is nothing like this, neither would I let it be. My world is the exact opposite in fact. It's filled with light, with God, with angelic forces that guide me to where I want to go. In my world I have a ray of heavenly light that surrounds and protects me. In my paradise the day starts at 6.30 a.m. with an hour walk around a beautiful country park where nature awes me with its beauty and where McDonald's awaits me at 7.30 a.m. with a lovely hot cup of coffee and the morning papers. At 9 a.m. my world gives me a beautiful huggy-kissy wife who greets me with a hearty (healthy) breakfast in a detached and converted house with its own gym. I have a kicking life, every day is Christmas, I can do what I want to do and achieve what I want to achieve. Do you want to know why it's so good and why it's getting better and better? Because

I make it so with *my* thoughts. I am the ruler of my world and I choose to make it one that is fit for me to live in.

Are there really devils and demons? Are there really angels of light? If you choose to believe there are, then of course there are. I choose to be happy, it's a conscious choice that I made some years ago and since I did my life has been one of constant joy. I did it by changing my thoughts, which in turn changed my mind.

The things I *can* change, if I feel that change will make them better, I change. The things I *can't* change, that are outside my circle of influence, I accept. Instead I change my perception of them so that they do not affect me. What you have to ask yourself is, 'Do I want to be happy or unhappy?' Once you have chosen, the job is a simple one, change all the things in your life that make you unhappy until you are surrounded by things that make you happy. Focus every day and every minute of the day on being happy, on choosing happy thoughts, on doing happy things, on reading happy or enlightening books and watching happy or enlightening films. When you go for a drink, go to places that make you feel good and avoid places that make you feel bad.

Do I sound idealistic? Good, that's how I want to sound because if we choose it this is an idealistic world. If you decide that the sky is falling in then the sky is falling in. One of my friends accused me of hiding from things that I didn't want to hear or see. He accused me of being frightened of 'what is out there'. What I hide from and what I am frightened of is the fact that if I choose to chase shadows and look at the perceived bleakness of the world it will become my world. Am I frightened of touching the cooker because it burns? You're damn right I am. Am I hiding from it and avoiding it for the same reason? No, I've just learned that playing with fire is detrimental to my health; it doesn't lead to fulfillment or happiness.

Thoughts are the building blocks of our mind, they create and destroy worlds, so choose your thoughts wisely and train your mind by practising every day to attract only greatness, leave the sky-is-falling-in thoughts to those who want to dwell in dark corners. Just reading this book will not give you control over your thoughts, no more than reading a book on classical guitar will allow you to play music. But it will show you how. The process is no different from driving a car, you learn as much about the art of driving as you can then you get into the driving seat and get out onto the roads. Once you've passed your test you have the option, if you choose, to take those skills to an advanced level with more practice and more instruction. Anyone can do it if they practise enough, but you won't learn from the back seat, you have to take the wheel. To change your mind you have to change your thought habits, and you do this by spending time each day correcting faulty internal dialogue. Every time you think negative, stop yourself and make yourself think positive and continue doing so until the negative thoughts have been starved to death and the positives have grown strong on a diet of regular use. To think bad thoughts is very easy, they float into your mind uninvited. To think good thoughts, however, takes daily practice and constant vigilance.

Influences
Our thoughts are not always our own, they are often intrinsically linked to those around us. We are surrounded by people who see the world as an unfair and unjust place, people who fall into the blame trap and give over their power to some exterior force. These types of people are not good influences, they are metaphoric sandbags to those of us who want to fly our balloons. Bearing this in mind, and if your intent is to become a self-leader, you have to start by choosing your influences wisely.

Our minds are often built (or burnt) as much by our external influences as by our internal ones. In fact, I'd go as far as to say that much of our internal influence is built by external stimuli. Internally you can weed out the bad and install the good; it is a simple though often lengthy but very worthwhile process. This will always be an increasingly difficult task though if your external influences are not good. It'll be like one step forward and two steps back. If your influences are constantly pulling you down then as likely as not, unless you change them in a hurry, *down* is exactly where you are going to slide. Take Liam for instance. We spent about an hour at the café talking about his plans to start his own business. He was very excited about the prospect of working for himself and giving up the regular nine-to-five that had been his prison for five years. He wanted my opinion; did I think he could do it?

By the time we had finished talking he was hot; he was going to change the world with his great ideas and concepts. He couldn't wait to get started. I was excited and pleased for him. He was/is a hugely talented man, he had already achieved some great personal goals in his life that had impressed me. The only goal at this point that had eluded him, was self-employment; being his own boss. He rang me a week later; the line was colder than a snowman's gonads. The enthusiasm of a week before had disappeared to be replaced by a cynicism that stole the energy right out of the air. He started the conversation by telling me that he'd had second thoughts about his business venture and then went on to insist that 'no business is worth sacrificing the youth of your children and the love of your wife for.'

Excuse me? Did I miss something here?

He was so set against going into business for himself that it was as though I was talking to a complete stranger. The entrepreneur of a week ago had vanished down my phone line. He actually sounded angry with me because I'd said his business idea was sound and by inference worth losing his wife and kids for. I had a good idea what was going on. 'Who've you been talking to, Liam?' I asked after minutes of beating round the bush.

'Well,' he said, almost embarrassed, 'I talked to a couple of guys at the gym and they told me that when they were in business for themselves they were working eighty hours a week and never got to see their kids and the . . .' blah-de-blah. I think you get the picture. What was a great idea, a revolutionary concept, had suddenly, over the space of seven days and a couple of negative conversations, become the worst idea known to man. His positive thoughts had been swamped by the negative words of others. The moment a new idea or concept is formed is a pivotal moment. When the lobster sheds his shell to grow he is free of his old shell but at the same time he is also vulnerable to prey because he is without protection. Negatives tend to fly in when one is growing and still unsure, so be very careful about sharing your ideas with others until they are fully formed, unless you really trust the people concerned, or you might find yourself, like Liam, aborting the flight before your wheels have even left the ground. If you do get negative feedback in the very early stages, or at any stage for that matter, you must forge ahead irrespective otherwise all may be lost.

We can have a great idea, a brilliant notion and then, for whatever reason, the enthusiasm goes and we wonder why we ever thought we could do it in the first place. Escher was dogged by this problem, he said, 'At times, when I feel very enthusiastic it just seems as though no one in the world has ever made anything so beautiful and important. Shortly afterwards (after starting a project)—a matter of hours—it suddenly looks useless and I am overcome by the utter pointlessness of all the pitiable fiddling. But having taken it on I continue the next day as though my very life depended upon it.'

I'm not saying that Liam should not do a little market research; in fact I would insist that he did. Neither am I saying he should not look at the pros and the cons of going it alone, I would expect no less. But if you want to go into business in a successful way don't just talk to people that have failed in business because all you're going to get are tales of woe and excuses from those who are unlikely to say, 'I failed because I did this or that wrong.' They are more likely to say, 'I failed because the world is unfair and because I didn't want to sacrifice my wife and kids.'

I failed because the world is unfair

If you want to be a champion swimmer, it's better to speak to a champion swimmer than some guy that does a few lengths of the local pool at the weekend. If you want to be a millionaire then hang around millionaires.

I was in Las Vegas this year with Chuck Norris and I asked him how he managed to overcome negative thoughts when first entering a new vocation. This is what he said:

'A lot of times people look at the negative side of what they feel they can't do. I always look on the positive side of what I can do. And when I got into the film business I didn't say,

"Look Chuck, you're thirty-four years old, you've had no acting experience, there's 16,000 unemployed actors in Hollywood, the average income of an actor is $5,000 a year." Now if I had looked at that side of it, the negatives, it would have probably made me give up. But I didn't, I said, "You know, since Bruce Lee has sadly died there's a gap there for a good, strong, positive, heroic image on the screen." And that's what I wanted to portray—a positive image. Because movies in the seventies were kind of negative movies, anti-hero type movies. And that's how I went for it and that's what saved me because my acting left a lot to be desired. But I think that the image I tried to portray on the screen, a strong, positive person, is what saved me and why people tolerated the poor acting.'

Another friend, Jim, is a brilliant playwright. His work has been on in the West End of London and on Broadway. One of his plays was made into a film, *Little Voice*, which made it to the Oscars. Yet when he started trying to sell his work quite a few theatres turned him down. If he had listened to them he might never have become one of the most respected writers on the planet.

I remember the story about when Kevin Keegan had a trial, as a young up-and-coming footballer, for Coventry City. Jimmy Hill, who was in charge at the time, told Kevin to get himself a proper job because he was too small to make it in professional football. Can you imagine being told by one of the most important men in your chosen field that you haven't got what it takes and to 'get a proper job'? That kind of advice is enough to kill a potential career deader than a motorway hedgehog. Did it kill Kevin Keegan's career? Did he listen to Jimmy 'the chin' Hill and allow negative thoughts to infiltrate his mind? No, because he knew what he had, he knew he was good, he believed in himself and felt that if he kept knocking doors eventually one would open. Mr Keegan went on to become one of the highest paid, highest profiled—and by all accounts one of the nicest—footballers in the history of the game. What you need to remember is that not everything you hear is true. Just because someone says you haven't got it doesn't make it law. So don't allow others' words to become your thoughts. Even the Beatles got turned down by an agent that said they'd never make the big time. In fact the agent's claim to fame now is that he turned down the Beatles.

Take advice, it's important, take constructive criticism, it'll help you to grow, but if anyone should ever tell you that you haven't got it, say, 'On your bike you nasty spanner,' then go on and prove them wrong.

If you don't like the mind you've got, change the thoughts in it for better ones and your mind will change all by itself.

48

Rule Four

How to get the energy for the journey

Reaching great heights and becoming who we want to become is great, it is what this book is all about, but there is a cost involved and that cost is energy, so Rule Four is about *'How to get the energy for the journey.'*

On any journey we need fuel or we're not going to get beyond the garden gate. Imagine you are going on a long journey in your car, what's the first thing you do? You fill the car up with fuel otherwise you're not going to get past the end of the street. Our journey through life is no different; we need fuel if we are to move from where we are to where we want to be.

Our energy in life comes from several things; the food we eat, the air we breathe and our influences. We also receive energy and empowerment from resisting the untrue, which means not doing the things that we know are wrong.

The food we eat is something most people don't think too much about, and I'm not about to get heavily into diet because it is peripheral to this book, only to say that 'we are what we eat'. There is also the Kabbalah belief that all of our energy and power is locked into our addictions, and once we kill those addictions we get all our energy and power back. I believe this to be true, certainly from my own experience. As we are all probably aware, one of the greatest addictions in this society is food, or more specifically, processed and so-called 'junk food'. We fill ourselves full of rubbish and then wonder where all of our energy goes. If we are not strong enough to resist a cigarette or a pint of beer how are we ever likely to be able to reach the heights and handle the altitude once we are there? Others have addictions to pornography (another trap) or drugs. These addictions—even if you don't really want to hear it (I certainly didn't)—are chains that tie us to an unfulfilled life. Once you sever them and use the energy to take you where you want to go you are destined for greatness. It took me many years to come to terms with this premise, in my ignorance I felt that I could do the things I wanted to do, handle the responsibility of realising my dreams and still have my addictions. I wanted to have my cake and to eat it. I was wrong and until I started to slay these addictions—in my case it was junk food—I never really got to second base. Once I did—first with alcohol, then with fast food—it was like the gates opened and everything started to happen for me.

Your head has to be right to get it though. I told one of my friends that I had given up beer and he nearly fell over. 'Well,' he scoffed, 'if I give up the beer I might as well stick my head in the oven and call it a day, I mean, what else is there if you give up the beer?'

Another friend in Wales said, 'I'll give up anything, other than beer. It's all we have here in Wales, that and sheep.' I used to think exactly the same, if I gave up my little treats what else was there? I felt sorry for myself and like most people do, 'a few beers won't hurt me'. And they're probably right, but if you want to go right to the top you have to make sacrifices, and for me that meant getting off the mat where I'd been rolling around with my training partners for thirty years and getting in a little cerebral sparring, fighting against my addictions, developing my weaker areas and perfecting my stronger ones. It meant leaving the physical arena behind because that's just primary school stuff compared with the fights you have, the small wars you encounter, in the old grey matter. Do you know how hard it is to resist a beer and a curry? Give me three rounds with Tyson any day of the week. Now I am not saying that if you don't give up beer or curry (or whatever) that you won't make it. Of course we all know lots of successful people who reach great heights and still enjoy these things, though often to the detriment of their health. But our addictions are the weak link in the chain and many greats have come plummeting down to the lower echelons

51

entirely because they indulged, and didn't kill their addictions. Abstinence is one way, and a very good way, of gaining the cerebral strength to climb the stairway to success and stay there. Messner, one of the great mountaineers of our day, said that climbing to the top of a perilous mountain was not his idea of a successful climb; living to tell the tale was.

A lot of the food that we consume these days does little more than clog the system, that's one of the areas where our energy is lost. The other area is our 'will'. If we cannot even resist a takeaway curry and a beer, how strong really is our will? Before you can lead a cavalry you have to be able to lead yourself, and you can't do that if you feel as though you look silly sitting on a horse. When I gave up alcohol it was to take back the power that was locked into my addiction, it was to clear my system of this drug and it was to exercise my will; the beer became a sparring partner on a cerebral level. I didn't do it so that I could tilt a lance at others who liked a drink. I'm not saying that alcohol is wrong for you; just that it is wrong for me. Since I killed my addiction my life has improved beyond measure. The strength I have gained or regained has enabled me to take many aspects of my life—not least my business—to greater heights.

Similarly, you can exercise your will by resisting any kind of food or drug or addiction. Gandhi eventually gave up sex in his bid to develop or reap back power. Gandhi developed such a strength of will via exercises in abstinence that, in the end, he had over 250 million followers. He'd never lifted a weight, never sparred with the Gracies, never built any kind of physical prowess, in fact he was against all forms of violence, all he did was develop an iron will by resisting and killing his addictions.

Again, we can only get out what we put in and if we fill ourselves with dietary rubbish, then our performance will be negated by our primary fuel supply. This body is the window through which we see the world, so it is very important that we keep it in good order. It is also very difficult to sustain any level of achievement if we lack energy and are constantly selling what energy we do have for a quick shot of addiction.

Maintaining a good diet is difficult; it has to be said that diet is the hardest discipline of all. Probably the ultimate discipline. But if you want to take this vehicle on a great journey, treat it regally and only put in the very best fuel. Cut out the junk food and start looking for healthy options.

Imagine that, for whatever reason, we, like our forefathers, were forced to live off the land, no shops or supermarkets, no takeaways etc. What would you eat? What would be available? That's the kind of food you should use as your dietary mainstay. And I have to tell

53

you that when you first start it is difficult, our addiction to the junk is a strong one, and the food that is good for you can seem very plain by comparison. However, once the addiction has been broken your body once again starts to crave the right stuff, you start to look forward to eating healthily, you even start looking for good food choices when you go out for a meal. Once the addiction has been broken for a short while, your body starts to reject the rubbish if you try to put it back in. Over one Christmas I decided to have a little treat (as I called it at the time), I had a couple of takeaways and some chocolate—well, quite a lot of chocolate. Afterwards my stomach was killing me and I felt mentally and physically clogged. I had not eaten it for so long that, in the end when I did try my body let me know immediately that it didn't like it. And here's the weird thing, even though the food made me feel ill I still craved it like crazy, the sight of a Mars bar and I'd be salivating.

We feel as though we can compromise with our addictions, that we can have a bit 'now and then', but in all honesty we either have a full-blown addiction or we do not. You can't have a bit of an addiction any more that you can be a bit pregnant. I know that sounds harsh, but you know it's true. And the time for you to kill these addictions of course is now. There is no other time. Now is the time, make the decision, write it down so that you are committed and do it now. Tomorrow is just a promissory note that might never be honoured.

This doesn't mean that you have to live like a monk, only that you should eat five-star, healthy: fruits, vegetables and fresh water to mention just three. Write down your addictions (be honest), and gradually lose them from your life, see what a huge difference it makes.

Physical training of some sort is also very beneficial if we want the body to work at peak performance. A lot of our energy can be trapped in a body that is log-jammed with residue stress hormones. Training flushes them out of the system; it clears the pipes so to speak. You don't have to become a world class athlete to do this—in fact I'd recommend that you didn't because most world class athletes over-train—just get in some good physical workouts every other day.

It is difficult, though not impossible, to choose the air we breathe because it tends to come with the environment in which we live, though of course we can choose/change our environment. But it is important because, as with the food, it is what we take in that determines what we get out. Ideally, if finances allow and if the environment in which we live is full of bad air, we should change it for one where the air is better. If this is not possible, try and take regular breaks to somewhere that offers good air. I get away every 4-8 weeks to Sherwood Forest for a few days just to top up on good, fresh unpolluted air. When I come back I feel brilliant, invigorated. It has affected me so much that I have already planned to buy a place with my own land so that I can bathe in good fresh air day and night. I want to be able to look out the window when I am writing and see fields and trees and because I know that it is within my power to do I will make it so.

It's slightly peripheral to this point but I remember reading Richard Branson's life story, *Keeping My Virginity*. What a great book and what a great man. He started with next to nothing and just went out there with the spirit of adventure and made it happen. He grabbed the world by the throat and shook it until he got what he wanted. Part-way through the book, not long after he had started Virgin Records, he went and looked at a beautiful country mansion. I remember reading and thinking, 'It sounds like a lovely place but there's no way he'll get a mortgage for it.' At the time, although he was doing well and his ambition was smashing glass ceilings to bits wherever he went, he just didn't have the financial muscle to take on such a big place. The next thing you know he's at the bank, convincing them that they should hand over the readies, and because his charisma and self-belief were the size of a small continent, he took the money and bought this fabulous mansion in the country with its own lake and land and all the trappings of millionairedom. I remember thinking, 'Wow!' A bit further into the book it happens again, only this time his eye fell on an island. Naïvely I thought again, 'It's a nice thought Mr Branson, and you are doing pretty well for yourself now, but an island? I don't think so.' I nearly fell off my chair and choked on my butter-less batch in the next page when the bank actually gave him the money and he bought an island. An island! Now I'm aware that this is an extreme example and that Mr Branson has bollocks the size of coconuts but the point remains; if he had taken the advice of others who were saying things like, 'No you fool!' and, 'You're mad!', he wouldn't be where he is now, he wouldn't be the most famous business tycoon on the face of the earth.

I digress.

If you think that the air we breathe doesn't affect who and what we are then you should try one of these breaks or ask the bank for enough money for your own island and see what a profound difference it makes. The first time Sharon suggested it to me I was falling apart, I had been working and training so hard that bits were falling off me, I was on the edge. I told her I doubted very much whether four days in a forest (even if Robin Hood had lived there once) would turn me around. 'And anyway,' I said, 'I've got too much to do, I can't afford to have four days away.'

'Geoff,' she said, in a way that only women can, 'looking at the state of you now, you can't afford not to have four days away.'

Needless to say we went. She can be very domineering at times.

You can't afford NOT to have a holiday

I took a four-day break to the forest and for the first two days I slept. I have never slept so much. When I finally came to from my much-needed slumber I went to the driving range and hit a few golf balls (the 'golfs' were not happy I can tell you), went for a lovely meal and talked in the bar over a cup of tea for hours. I felt brilliant, revitalised, and not just for the duration of the holiday but for months after. The moment I arrived home I booked another break for eight weeks' time, this gave me something to work to (and for). I realised on that break that to succeed in all aspects of life you need to keep in constant balance, you have to work hard, rest hard and play hard, if any of these elements are missing your balance is out. As I sit here writing this book now I feel pretty tired and ready for a break, but because I have another one booked very soon (again in Sherwood Forest), I can push through the tiredness because I know that before long I'll be able to hit golf balls, eat beautiful and healthy meals and read books—and the air will be kicking.

Holidays by the sea are also great; there is nothing quite like sea air to rejuvenate and empower you. I was recently in Plymouth, a lovely city, on a book-signing tour and I deliberately booked a hotel that overlooked the sea; it was awesome. We walked along the beach for two hours before I did my talk in the bookshop and we couldn't believe the beauty and expanse of the sea. The air was so fresh that it was hard not to be energised. The next day I awoke at about 6 a.m., left Sharon in bed and walked down the beach again. I couldn't resist. It was pitch-black and blowing a gale but I had to go. Unfortunately I had forgotten my hat so I made my own using an old cotton tea towel (I looked a bit of a spanner). I got to the seafront in seconds, it was freezing but I didn't care, I wanted to experience the power and majesty of the sea again before we got the train back that morning. It was very dark still, there were hundreds of seagulls flying above me, the waves were pounding against the sea walls and I was in heaven. It was the greatest feeling, one that I intend to repeat more in the future. The sea! Brilliant air. Get it if you can.

On a more immediate level, try to avoid smoke-filled areas like pubs, clubs, bars etc. where all you do is take rubbish into your lungs. Don't tolerate others smoking around you; if it is within your power to stop them or to change the environment then do so.

I believe it was William Blake, the great poet, who said, 'The eagle never lost so much time, as when he submitted to learn off the crow.' We are eagles, so why do we listen to crows when they spout their negative advice/critique?

This is a biggie and a subject I have already touched upon.

More energy is created and/or stolen by the influences that we allow into our lives than anything else. And our influences are many fold.

You might not realise it but our immediate environment (where we actually live) is responsible for a lot of our energy. Our environment influences our behaviour. Being surrounded by grey walls and uninspiring locales can dampen our ardour quicker than an injection of 'pull-me-downs'. So brighten up the rooms you live in and, if you can, the place in which you work. Bang up a few inspirational posters conveying words of wisdom. Even the dashboard of your car can be plastered with inspiring quotations. My locker at work (when I worked) was lined with photos of those that inspired me most. My home is always brightly decorated, great music can be heard playing in the background, and I have great books by great people adorning nearly every room. Pictures by Escher are on my study walls and books on Steinberg, another great artist, and Michelangelo are sat on my reading room table. Even the toilet has magazines with positive articles ready for reading. I try to make everything around me positive and inspiring. My house is filled with great books, which are amongst the most inspiring items you can own. Books change my world and just having them around fills me with glee.

You control your environment, so if it doesn't lift you then change it until it does. Surround yourself with greatness if it is greatness that you are looking for.

However, don't blame your environment or

anything else for your failures. As I said before blame is a trap, once you blame, you hand over your power.

When I was younger my environment was just one of the things I used to rationalise my failure. I'd say things like, 'If I didn't live around here I could really do something with my life,' or, 'there are no opportunities to get on in this city.'

I'd blame anything and everything, not knowing at the time that when we blame we give over our power, when we blame we take away our ability to change our luck. How can we change something if we don't even accept that it is our responsibility? Like the alcoholic, we cannot even begin to deal with our problems until we first accept that the problems are ours to deal with. Maxwell Maltz the great motivational writer and speaker, in his classic book *Psycho-Cybernetics* says that:

'This new concept (of taking the reins and accepting responsibility) does carry a responsibility, however. No longer can you derive sickly comfort from blaming your parent, society, your early experiences, or the injustices of "others" for your present troubles. These things may and should help you understand how you got where you are. Blaming them, or even yourself for the past mistakes, however, will not solve your problem, or improve your present or your

future. There is no merit in blaming yourself. The past explains how you got here. But where you go from here is your responsibility. The choice is yours. Like a broken phonograph, you can keep on playing the same old "broken record" of the past; re-living past injustices; pitying yourself for past mistakes; all of which reactivates failure patterns and failure feelings which colour your present and your future.

Or, if you choose, you can put on a new record, and reactivate success patterns and "that winning feeling" which help you do better in the present and promise a more enjoyable future.

When your phonograph is playing music you don't like, you do not try to force it to play better. You do not use effort or will power. You do not bang the phonograph around. You do not try to change the music itself. You merely change the record being played and the music takes care of itself.'

Some of the greatest success stories of our time are about men and women who came from the very worst type of background. Julian Richer, of Richer Sounds, is worth an estimated £50 million and his advice is sought by Chief Executives of some of Europe's biggest organisations, his ideas on staff motivation have been described by the national press as 'legendary', yet he started out as a working class lad, a 'poor performer at school'. Jim Cartwright, one of the best-known and respected playwrights produced in England, had an uninspiring comprehensive education and left school with little or no prospects. The legacy his father left him was that he could do 'anything you set your mind on.' He proved his dad right when his plays were a smash in the West End and on Broadway. His background was a working class, two-up-two-down terrace in the north of England. His environment did not stop him from becoming great, but it could have if he'd let it. I'm not saying that these people automatically made it to the top, they made many mistakes on their way up, as we all do. But don't worry about making mistakes, quite often it is our errors that make us who we are, and often mistakes can lead to great discoveries. Columbus only found America by mistake when he was trying to find a quick route to India. Wernher von Braun said that it takes 6,500 errors before you can make a rocket. Edison, the inventor of the light bulb, failed thousands of times but said he had found thousands of ways how not to make a light bulb. Laminated glass was first produced by accident and it has since saved the lives of thousands, and Colonel Sanders was turned down no less than 1,009 times. Mistakes are what we make on the way to becoming great.

Guided missiles work solely by going off track. When the information is sent back they are put back on track again. This continues until the target has been found.

Make mistakes. Learn from them, they are part of the weathering process.

Edison failed many times before he invented the light bulb

There is an old Nordic belief that the North Wind made the Vikings. If they had not endured bitter winters and freezing winds they might never have developed the hardiness that the inclement weather tempered in them. If your environment is hardy, if your background is one of strife, if you feel that providence has left you at the bottom of a long ladder, then I say good, if there is no adversity there is no advance. There is nothing like a challenge to spur you on to greatness and nothing like a dose of complacency to kill your dreams. Use your environment to climb the ladder; your environment often is the ladder. The adversity of having everything against you is just the motivation you need to get to the top. Someone like Muhammad Ali would certainly not be the man he is today if he had not been brought up on a diet of poverty and prejudice; his environment made him probably the best-known sportsman of the entire species. And he wasn't born a great fighter; he had to develop his skills. He wasn't born with a fast jab and fancy footwork, he trained himself to greatness. Similarly, Gandhi used his environment, his disposition and his colour to make himself the greatest leader for peace and unity—in my view—this world has ever seen. Mother Teresa—as close to sainthood as one can get—was brought up in very humble surroundings and in fact spent her life in absolutely abhorrent conditions and environments—but it didn't stop her from becoming the most recognised and respected woman on the face of the Earth.

Your environment can only hold you back if you let it. If you focus on a goal and use every part of you to make that goal a reality there is nothing that will or can stop you. You'll be surprised (a strange but true fact) at the readiness with which the world steps aside—or comes to your aid—in carrying out that goal once your mind is set. I have found that once I commit to something, and I do mean fully commit, it's as though the universe conspires to help me bring my dream to fruition. To make my commitment real I always write it down on a piece of paper and date it. Once written down with full commitment I have always attained my aims, and serendipity always clears my path and lends a hand.

Many people use their environment as a scapegoat for their shortcomings, 'If it wasn't for where I lived I could really do something with my life,' is a usual complaint. If you are not happy with your environment then change it, you have the ability to do this. If people spent as much energy on seeking solutions as they did on procrastinating, their problems would vanish and their world would be alive instead of slumbering or dead.

The Branson mentality

You wouldn't believe the things that some of my friends achieve. It's incredible, and it's inspiring. Carl, for instance, has just bought a £350,000 house complete with its own lake. You'd think that the lad was rich, but he's not. He has a good job—he fits windows—and his wife works in a local supermarket. Just an ordinary couple really. What makes them different from the majority is that they have what I like to call the *'Branson mentality'*. That is, they see what they want and, irrespective of what obstacles might be in their way, they set out to get it. And they always do. While most people might be spending their money on cigarettes and drink, going out for meals or wasting it on things that give them no return, this pair invest every penny of what they earn—and much of their time—into their house. What they love more than anything else is to sit on the patio of their beautiful house with a cup of tea and look out into their own lake.

I drive a nice car and own a lovely house too. My friend Steve said to me one day, 'I'd love to have a house and a car like yours.'

I said, 'Steve, if you'd love to have it then have it.' He looked back at me as though I'd just landed a spacecraft on his fuchsias.

'I can't afford all this.' I thought he was going to cry. I told him he could afford it, he was earning enough money and he had the capacity to earn more, it was just what he did with what he earned that left him broke most weeks. I sat with him for half an hour and we worked out what he actually did earn and where he spent it. When the figures were in black and white he nearly fell off his chair. What he spent each week on partying and going out worked out to be one and a half times the amount he needed to have the house and the car of his dreams. He was spending hundreds just at the weekend. The irony was that probably two thirds of what he was spending he didn't even remember because he was so drunk. One Friday, before he went to the pub, he left a couple of hundred pounds in another pair of trousers, money to last him through the week. He got so drunk at the weekend that he couldn't remember where he'd left it. After searching in all the wrong places for the money and not finding it (he eventually did) he concluded that he 'must have spent it at the weekend.' Now you might call me highly perceptive, you might even think that I'm a raving mathematical genius but if he can lose £200 and just presume that he'd spent it on 'dolly mixtures and sherbet', how much was he actually spending in the first place? He argued that the weekends were the only time that he had to relax, all he had to look forward to after working a hard week. I argued back that he didn't have to get 'rat-faced' to have a good time and if he did, perhaps he should take a closer look at his life. I don't mean to sound judgmental here because I have led this kind of existence myself. I'm trying to be objective and say, 'If you are given the choice between the stars and a heap of dog dung why take the shit, why set your sights so very low?' If a guy comes up to you in the pub and says, 'Nudge, nudge, wink, wink, got a little deal for you. I can give you— gratis, free of charge, on the house—a million dollars or this lovely piece of dog's crap that I just shovelled off the pavement,' what are you gonna choose? Call me greedy, accuse me of being materialistic but, and this is just a personal view, I'll take a permanent rain-check on the dog shit.

This is not to say that all riches are of the

materialistic genre. My greatest riches can't be measured by the car I drive or the balance in my bank. Those are pretty meaningless compared to my health, my beautiful wife, my gorgeous kids, and the fact that I still have my parents. And what a great life I have. Every morning I wake up and thank God for another day because I am so happy, I love being me, I am so grateful (not lucky, you make your own luck by meeting providence half-way up the road instead of waiting for him to knock on your door) to live the life of a writer, sculpting a service through the letters of the alphabet. It's a pleasure, I have to say. The key with the materialistic side of it is to enjoy it—and I do—but not to attach to it, never make money your God because if you do, believe me you'll be very disappointed. This doesn't mean that you have to run away from wealth, there's nothing wrong with having money, profit is healthy, it's how we live, even the Bible needs money to pay the printing bills. But I never look for money to make me happy, on its own it is about as inspiring as a dung beetle. If you can put the money to work for the better good of others, give some back in other words, then money becomes an organiser that can help you to help others to help themselves. I look at some of the great entrepreneurs and, without exception, the ones that are happiest are those that invest their wealth in others. People like Julian Richer are great philanthropists; he gives one day in every seven to help others without a profit. Richard Branson constantly lavishes money on investing for the better good of others. The happiest people of all the great success stories I have read are those that invest their wealth by giving back, by doing for others with no thought of a profit.

The law of compensation
And this is another great way—probably the very best—to gain energy; give it away (what are you saying you crazy fool!). No it's true. What you give is what you get. This is the law of compensation that says cast your bread out onto the waters and it will return tenfold.

There are people out there that make a great living just helping others to make theirs. One guy I read about did nothing but help people get in touch with others that might need their service. If you needed a plumber he'd give you the number of a plumber that'd look after you. If you needed pallets he'd know the man with enough pallets to give you some for free. He helped so many people and so many people loved him because he did it all for free that, when they had a great tip on a business venture, or stocks of 'blah-de-blah' going cheap, they'd ring him and give him the nod. When he received great tips he acted upon them and made his fortune.

Giving is good, and for this particular

gentleman that was all he did. He did it because he had faith in the law of compensation; he knew that what he gave always came back to him—in even greater abundance. He believed it to such an extent that he actually felt selfish when he gave to others because he knew it was all coming back like a bet that he couldn't lose, an investment that always gave a good return. He saw giving as a reciprocal experience, where both he and the person he had given to both benefited. In a sense giving is a selfish act, or what Charles Handy would call 'proper selfishness', giving and receiving, but giving with no thought of return. Once you start looking for any kind of profit it stops being a gift and instead becomes a conditional offering, 'I'll give to you, but only on account that you give back to me.' When you expect something back it becomes a deal, and once it carries conditions it lacks love and the law of compensation no longer applies. When I give I expect nothing in return, and every time I give it comes back in abundance, maybe not directly from the person I have given to, and maybe not immediately but it always returns and with profit. The danger of expecting back when you give is that it courts cynicism, suddenly when the return is not forthcoming you become bitter and protest about how unfair and unjust people are and how, in fact, the law of compensation does not work because you tried it. The law of compensation only works when you completely detach yourself from profit. You know the return will be there, but you don't look for it. You give for the better good of others, knowing that all that is given in faith will return, but not caring whether it does or not because the mere satisfaction of giving is reward enough. Initially it is hard not to think 'if I help so-and-so I know it'll be beneficial to me', it's human nature. But with practice it'll get easier and easier, you'll give so much that in the end you'll have forgotten whom you have given to, so when it all comes back to you it'll be a complete surprise.

I once worked for a guy who spent every weekend away from work slaving on the farm of an old gentleman he had met during the Second World War. When his mates told him he was mad to slave away for nothing, he gave them a sly wink and said, 'The old guy'll be dead in a few years and if I look after his farm and work for nothing he's bound to leave it all to me, he's got no family in this country.' As he predicted the man did die, though not as quickly as he would have liked, but he didn't leave the farm to him, rather he left it to a charity for cats. My workmate was so angry and spent the remaining years until he himself died complaining about how selfish the old fellow was and what an unjust world it all is.

If you do it for the wrong reasons your return will always be disappointment. Also, by

74

giving only to receive you pawn your power to a promissory note that never appears. An old girlfriend said to me, 'Giving to others does nothing but leave you in a mess, I have given to others and look at the mess I am in now, I'm depressed and alone.' She believed that she was in a mess because others had not returned her kindness; she was in a mess because she expected a return, and when it did not come she became disappointed, then disillusioned, then depressed and alone. I expect nothing, I want nothing, that's why it always comes. But as I said—and I'm in danger of labouring the point here—the return often does not come from the people you give to, the magic, the beauty is that it can and might come from anywhere at any time but rest assured it will come. The art is learning to give for the love of giving and get off on giving. Make giving your apple pie and custard, your Sunday pint, your night by the telly, your grapple on the mat, your early night, your lie-in, your summer hols. Do it again and again until you make it a habit. You'll have so much joy in your life you'll be overflowing with the stuff.

What an epitaph to have engraved in marble, don't you think, wouldn't you agree: 'He was legendary for giving to others.' That's the kind of epitaph that makes a man immortal. One of my great heroes—you'll probably hear his name throughout this book—was a man called George Julius Hackenschmidt, a legendary wrestler before the Great War. I have read many stories of this great man's capacity for strength and wrestling but none impressed me so much as the stories I read and heard about his legendary capacity for giving to others.

Plant your seeds
Giving is just one of the ways of acquiring fuel for the journey, but we still have to travel that journey and this is where many people fail. They get bundles of energy, bags of seeds, but they don't use it or plant them, they just sit surrounded by their potential.

Invariably the energy then overwhelms them. The natural power we possess does not fare well with idleness. It's like filling a tank with petrol and not using any, eventually if you keep filling, the tank will overflow. This is where people start to displace their energy—because they have too much—in a negative way. So collect the seeds and then make sure you plant them well. To do this again means being proactive, get out there and do it, lead don't follow, create don't copy. And keep your influences positive.

The great Og Mandino in his book *The Greatest Salesman in the World* advises us to become great by leading and not following:

'I will persist until I succeed. I am not delivered unto this world in defeat, nor does failure course through my veins. I am not a sheep waiting to be prodded by my shepherd. I am a lion and I refuse to talk, to walk, to sleep with the sheep. I will hear not those who weep and complain, for their disease is contagious. Let them join the sheep. The slaughterhouse of failure is not my destiny. Failure I may still encounter at the thousandth step, yet success hides behind the next bend in the road. Never will I know how close it lies unless I turn the corner. I will persist with the knowledge that each failure to sell will increase my chance for success at the very next attempt. Each "nay" I hear will bring me closer to the sound of "yea". Each frown I meet only

*prepares me for the smile to come. Each
misfortune I encounter will carry in it the
seed of tomorrow's good luck. I must have
night to appreciate the day. I must fail often
to succeed only once.*
I will persist until I succeed.'

Step into the unknown

Our journey invariably means seeking out
lions and avoiding sheep. We have
emphatically to refuse to be sheep, we have
the choice and we should choose high. When
we are given the choice between the mud and
the stars, we'd be fools to take the mud. Be
bold, insist on thinking big, what we think is
what we become, but we need consistency with
our thoughts and this takes constant and daily
practice. What we don't use we lose, the
moment we take our attention away from our
positive thoughts negative thoughts start to
grow. A garden will be overrun with weeds in a
heartbeat if it is not constantly managed. What
we focus on becomes our future, and what we
do not focus on becomes our past.

Step into the unknown, break down comfort
zones and seek new pastures, find and/or
realise your goal. To do this we must swim
against the stream, be prepared to step into
adversity, face down our own fears, go (as they
say) where others fear to tread. It also means
swimming against the societal stream, the

opinion of others. Once you swim against the stream (and this is one of life's paradoxes) you can go with the universal flow. I found that initially when I started to go my own way, I felt alone and scared.

Go where others fear to tread

And every time I stopped for a breather other 'fish' would say, 'What are you going that way for? That's the wrong way, come with us you blighter.' However, it wasn't long before I started to attract others with a similar philosophy to my own, others that didn't want to be sheep and follow the crowd. Invariably these people would offer me advice and support and I'd offer some back, all of a sudden I didn't feel so alone any more. It is then that you no longer have to 'fight', you just have to let go and trust the sway.

Sigmund Freud once said, 'I have discovered long since that it only needs a little courage to fulfil wishes which till then have been regarded as unobtainable.' Courage is the one thing that most people seem to lack when it comes to chasing goals. Everyone wants a no risk situation, everyone wants a guarantee. Well, one thing I do know is that there is never a guarantee. I have dealt with many people in my life and the majority suffered from this infuriating ailment: 'Well, there's no guarantee that it's going to work.' Well of course there isn't, that's why the leaders are out there all on their own having the booty to themselves, that's the reason why 95 per cent of the wealth in this country (in most countries) lies with only 5 per cent of the people. Because that 5 per cent don't need a guarantee. They just get out there and ride the bull. There is always a chance that you might fall off, and often you do, but life allows you to get right back on again and have another try. And the beauty is that if/when you fall off, you learn a hell of a lot about 'falling' that you can use the next time you ride the bull. And you know what they say, if you fall, pick something up. It is all about having a positive philosophy and a permanent and strong grip on your thoughts. We should not seek never to fall, rather we should seek always to rise after falling.

In his book *Master Key to Riches*, Napoleon Hill has a great philosophy about positive thinking. When thanking providence, God, the Universe (whatever) for all his happiness and wealth he says:

> 'My gratitude to you also for revealing to me the truth that no human experience need become a liability; that all experiences may be transmuted into useful service; that the power of thought is the only power over which I have complete control; that the power of thought may be translated into happiness at will; that there are no limitations to my power save only those which I set up in my own mind.'

No one ever got anywhere different by following the same path as the masses. Seek your own path, the one, as they say, that is least travelled.

Fighting fear
I can give you bags and bags of fuel, you can collect it by the bagful yourself, you can grow it

81

by the ton but of what use is it if you are too afraid to get into the car and drive? So the next piece in the jigsaw is fighting the fear that stops you from getting out onto the road. Notice the things that others will not or cannot do, these are what you need to do. Notice the path that others feel is unreasonably hard; this should be the path you take. Check out the work ethic that the majority feel too demanding, take on this work ethic and more. On the road less travelled there are no seasons; we don't do less because it's a bit cold, or a bit hot, because it rains, or because the snow is falling. No seasons, just a progressive work ethic. If you want more than the rest then work harder than the rest and face the things that the rest are afraid to face. Get angry with yourself when that negative voice tells you that the road is hard, get mad and get on with the journey, remind yourself that is has to be hard, it has to be a difficult road, if it isn't you will not grow. Discomfort is a sign of growth, knowing that this is a truth can bring great solace, it will allow you to be comfortable in your discomfort.

This is also where you will acquire secondary energy because each time you face a fear and step into adversity your self-esteem (an energy gift from the super ego, your internal parent) will grow, and each time you get a success behind you, you become more confident of overcoming the next hurdle. In the end, with a series of successes littering your trail, you start to understand and believe that there is nothing you cannot do, nothing you cannot achieve, no place you cannot go, no one you cannot become. Your belief system expands to previously unthinkable parameters. Every time you overcome a new obstacle you metamorphose, you become a brand new person, you become bigger, like the lobster you grow into a new and bigger shell which you will eventually also crack to reform another and another and yet another. Don't be a crab stuck in the fisherman's basket believing the prison to be a home. Don't pull others back when they want to escape the basket and don't be pulled back by the other crabs yourself. Do not be a follower awaiting the instructions or dictations of those above, you are a leader, a person that makes his or her own decisions and cuts his or her own path. If you want to be great then think great, and act great then you'll be great.

Byron Janis said that, 'The mind, like the universe, is ever expanding. And the mind, like the universe, has no limits.' Unless you impose your own. If your biggest thought is being the foreman in the local factory then you are very unlikely to ever grow beyond that station. Aim for the stars; at least then if you miss you still get the moon. If you struggle to think like the mountain then think a bit smaller, make your thoughts a reality and then immediately think of the next level you want to attain. You have to choose a better and bigger way to live, be prepared to take every risk and embrace every opportunity that may provide a better life.

That's the thing that really excites me, that there is no end to our potential, our consciousness can grow to infinite levels, it is only limited by fear and we only fear the things that we do not know. As we expand our knowledge so our fears dispel and our consciousness grows. Knowledge is like a growth hormone for the consciousness.

So look at where you want to go, get the fuel and start the journey. The fear that you feel initially is soon dispelled; it only exists on the edges of our comfort zone, as soon as we crash through that fear will go. It always does. Every time you grow a new shell, crack it open while it is still malleable and move onto the next shell and so on until eventually there will be no shell big enough to hold you.

I'll end this chapter with the immortal words of Seneca who said that, 'It is not because things are difficult that we dare not, it is because we do not dare that they are difficult.'

Rule Five

The power is yours alone

Life offers options and it's down to us to choose the right one. And don't think that you haven't got the choice because you have, we all have. To think that we haven't is to place ourselves in a victim state; it's like handing over all our power, all our freedom to some outside influence because we think we have to. So Rule Five is: *'The power is yours alone.'* You're in charge, it's your life, and this is your world, your incarnation, and your time to either spend investing in your dreams or living your worst reality. If every single thing about your life is wrong then change every single thing in it until it's right, and do it now because, as I said earlier—and forgive me for bringing it back up again—you're dying, we all are, so tomorrow is far too late. Start now, make plans, grab life by the throat and make it so.

If you're temporarily stuck in a life that doesn't offer the energy that you require, or it steals your energy and you can't move to a better environment immediately, then change the one you have for the better until you can. If you are truly stuck, and we very rarely are, handle it until you become unstuck, some of the greatest men and women in history created their genius in terrible environments.

Think of Robinson Crusoe and make the very best of what you have. If you have the *why* (why you want to do something) you will find the *how*, nothing will get in your way if you really want something; if you are not totally committed to the task everything will become an excuse to fail. Always avoid the people in a hurry to tell you that your idea stinks. Mark Twain warned that we should, 'Keep away from people who try to belittle your ambitions. Small people always do that, but the really great make you feel that you, too, can become great.'

Isn't that the truth! Negative people steal from us if we let them. They do, they actually come into our lives and nick our energy. 'Hello,' they say, 'I'll have a piece of that.' Then they're off, leaving you like a wilting wallflower. Negative people are like little tornadoes—they rush into our lives, blow the roofs off our houses and then disappear again without a by-your-leave, without a please, a thank you, a kiss my arse, nothing. In, big tornado, nick your dinner and out again. They leave you raped of all energy. And it's our own fault because we let them do it. They are responsible for stealing more of our energy than any other single factor—and we let them. But we shouldn't because the power is ours.

You can be feeling on top of the world,

ready to take on Goliath, to run the race, fight the fight, when BANG! Suddenly, out of the blue and often completely unprovoked, someone says something negative and steals the wind right out of our sails. One of my friends, a very positive man, told me that he often came down for breakfast in the morning feeling brilliant and ready for a very productive day. He felt as though nothing could dampen his spirits, he was floating on air excited about a new day . . . until his mother said, 'What harebrained scheme are you up to today?' And it flattened him like a shadow. Even his cornflakes went soggy. So much so that he thought to himself, 'What's the point of it all?'

They say that you can choose your friends but you can't choose your family. This is true of course, we can't choose our family but we can choose how we allow them to speak to us.

Luckily my family are very positive but if they were not I'd ask them either to speak positively to me or not speak to me at all. 'Mum,' I'd say, if she wasn't positive with me, which she is (thanks Mum), 'Mum, get your positive head on or I'm going to have to trade you in for a newer model.' Most people do not realise the power of their words, they don't really know that a harsh word can be like a hammer in the eye. So it is up to us to help our family and friends to be more supportive so that they might help and not hinder our aspirations. We have to stand our ground and say, 'Actually, I'm not having you speak to me like this.' We must tell them how their words cut and how sad they make us feel and that every bad word they fling at us erodes the love we feel. At one point in my life I did let someone walk all over me. But I eventually found a lady (Sharon) that liked my soft nature, nay she was attracted to it, and didn't feel the need to control.

People only treat us the way we allow them to

I believe that people only treat us the way we allow them to. If we just sit there and take it then, of course, they are going to disrespect us all day long. If however we stop the rot and say, 'Actually, I'm not having this any more,' then the chances are they'll stop or we'll move on.

What we must remember is that we are all a part of each other's comfort zone, so if you start to achieve and subsequently move from or expand that comfort zone, it will affect those around you. You will leave a vacuum in their life and they'll feel uncomfortable. Their way of coping with this is to drag you back by means of negative criticism. Don't have any of it. Demand support or move on. Give them plenty of chances if you can, help them to grow with you, don't just leg it at the first sign of conflict. But once you have satisfied yourself that they will not change then there is only one thing to do.

Our friends are often worse than our family because they also feel abandoned when we 'move up'. If you think enough of them you'll try and take them with you, though this can prove very difficult, you can't make people grow. People cannot be forced, they have to want it and earn it, and it's a very individual thing. Try and explain to them that you don't like their negative attitude and that they are pulling you down, ask them to change. Inevitably if they refuse you'll have to leave them behind or they'll hold you back. Don't worry too much, if you've tried your best to help them and they won't be helped then it's not your fault. When they are ready to grow try to be there for them. Until that time comes, move on.

George Bernard Shaw said that, 'People are always blaming their circumstances for what they are, the people who get on in the world are the people who get up and look for the circumstances that they want and if they can't find them, make them.'

Negative people will drag you down; they will make you feel as though you cannot achieve anything in life. And once you believe it, it'll become your truth.

So choose your friends wisely, help your family to support you or, if they cannot be helped, simply do not involve them in your aspirations. If someone makes you feel bad and they refuse to change, lose him or her from your life. As I said, and this needs to be reiterated, this doesn't mean that we run away every time someone has something bad to say, on the contrary, we should always exhaust mediation before we resort to separation. Talk and communicate until you are sure there are no other options. In my early relationships I sometimes spent years trying to help my partners grow because I didn't want to leave them behind. Give them every opportunity, talk with them, tell them how much you love them, how much their criticism hurts and that you fear losing them if they don't change. Also, you should always give them the chance to be right. Sometimes what people offer is good critique, even if it is delivered with aggression, and this can help us if we are open to suggestion. Sometimes they are right, and we have to make sure we are completely honest with ourselves before we kick them out of our lives. When I first got together with Sharon I was often guilty of this. She would offer what turned out to be good critique and I would accuse her of being negative towards me when in fact all she was trying to do was help. There is a big difference between negative and positive criticism, between criticism and critique. Make sure you take the time to get to know the difference.

I can't tell you how often, as a younger man, I let people pull me down, as though I was duty-bound. Friends, or so-called, would leave me feeling bad for days, and lo and behold, next time they called I'd let them do the very same again. I know I should have stood up to them but I didn't want the hassle or the embarrassment of speaking my mind. Now I have changed totally. I won't have it. I refuse to be a rubbish bin for other people's insecurities and I am very quick to let people know if I don't agree with what they have to say. 'Always be ready to speak your mind,' Blake advised, 'and a base man will avoid you.'

It's true, when you are honest with those that do not have your best interests at heart they will soon move on.

If you do take the critique in good faith make sure that it is meant to help your aspirations and not to hinder them.

You don't have to go very far to find your greatest influence, the person that either takes us to the stars or kicks us in the inspirational spuds. Ourselves. We are the ones with the power, with the ability to make it so.

When we do something good we feel pleased with ourselves, this empowers us and gives us energy, but when we let ourselves down by doing bad we punish ourselves with lowered self-esteem and poor self-worth. Basically we penalise ourselves for our wrongs by taking away energy. With this in mind it is important that we take a long, hard and honest look at ourselves and realise that we are the only ones to blame if things go wrong, it is our reality, our incarnation and we have the power—if only we realise it—to do what we will with our lives.

Rule Six

If your mind is not right, change it for one that is

You've probably heard the fable that says a leopard never changes its spots, and that people can't change. I have to tell you it's a lie. I am surrounded by people that are constantly changing who they are for who they would like to be. Almost like living several incarnations in the one lifetime. So Rule Six is: *'If your mind is not right, change it for one that is.'* One thing I have learned and one thing I know is that you can do anything.

People like Mahatma Gandhi, my hero, spent his whole life 'changing his mind'. His greatest source of inspiration was himself. He learned to talk himself into positive states of courage and inspiration by controlling his own thoughts. President Eisenhower, one of history's greatest leaders, wrote down on a piece of paper all the things about himself that he didn't like. He then set about improving on his weaknesses. When he first started this exercise in personal discipline, he had a long list (over fifteen items) of 'things to change and improve'. He highlighted and erased all the personality traits he felt would hold him back. Eventually, by systematically working through the list, he got it down to three. Then he worked hard at eradicating these also, until eventually he had replaced all his bad habits with good habits. That's how he became a very powerful man.

Similarly, Gandhi worked from a very early age to develop self-control so that he could lead himself and then others. He did this by practising abstinence. By controlling what he ate, what he thought, what he said and what he did—even down to his sex life, which he eventually gave up (I think a man can go too far!). This very slight, amiable Indian man became so powerful that he changed the course of history. At the time of his death this legendary pacifist had over twenty million followers. Twenty million people followed Gandhi because he had mastered what they could not. He mastered only one thing—himself. He had developed true power, the ability to control himself, the ability to get himself to do the things that he most wanted to do—even when he was scared to do it—and also the ability to stop himself from doing the things that he knew he should not. He was an awe-inspiring man.

People often look at the likes of Gandhi and say, 'Oh yeah, but that's Gandhi, I'm not gifted like him.' They look up to their icons and believe that these men are born with something they are not. In doing this, in placing their heroes on a pedestal they literally place their achievements beyond mortal reach, beyond their own reach. 'Only people like Gandhi can change the world,' they tell themselves. But Gandhi was not born with anything extra, what he had learned, he worked for. As a young man he struggled even to make a living as a not-very-successful lawyer. In fact he did not win a case for over two years. He was so unsuccessful at one point in his life that his parents despaired; they feared he might never make a living. He was an ordinary man who used his body and mind to become extraordinary. He is historic proof that one can 'change their mind' even if they start with very little.

History is full of so-called no-hopers who went on to change the world. William Wallace was only one man but after witnessing an atrocity—a village of women and children being raped and slaughtered—he decided to do extraordinary things. And he did, he changed the course of history by gathering an army and fighting back against an oppressive and bullying enemy. He became so legendary, even in his own lifetime, that people thought he must be a seven-foot tall monster that ate babies for breakfast. But he wasn't. He was a rather ordinary man of average build and intelligence who used every sinew of his being to change his mind and fight his cause. Now, many years after his death, they've even made a Hollywood movie about him (*Braveheart*, starring Mel Gibson). Walter Chrysler, the great American industrialist, began his working life as a mechanic in a railroad shop in Salt Lake City, Utah. He was not weaned for greatness; he did not have the mind of a history-changing mogul. He had no appreciable amount of working capital when he started, other than a few thousand dollars he had saved himself, his education was very limited and he had no wealthy backers to set him up in business, but he did have a practical idea and the initiative to change himself from an ordinary mechanic to an extraordinary industrial leader. He had a vision that the automobile industry had a future, when others merely saw the car as a weekend toy for the filthy rich. His entry into the car business was dramatic and quite novel. He spent his saved capital on a brand new car. He had the car delivered to his home and then promptly stripped it. Once the car was in pieces on his garage floor he set about rebuilding it only to strip it and rebuild it again and again until he knew the car—its strengths and weaknesses—like no one else. He took the car apart so many times that his mates thought he'd lost the plot. And from that experience he began to design his own automobiles, embodying the good points of the car he had taken to pieces and omitting the weaknesses. He did such a good job that when the Chrysler cars reached the market they became an overnight sensation. His rise to fame and fortune was huge and immediate and the Chrysler car became a household name. Mr Chrysler had every reason not to succeed and if he'd chosen he could have used them all as valid reasons why he might not succeed. But he didn't and the local garage mechanic with a poor education developed his mind to become the biggest thing in automobile history. All he started with was a good idea and a lot of tenacity. We all have at least that and if we choose—and I mean really choose—we too can change our world, and if we like—the whole world.

Start local

Before we can change the world we first have to change ourselves—we need to localise our first-aid. This often means having to mend our own faults, but before we can do this of course we have first to admit them, if only to ourselves. Many of us cannot bear to see the truth; the brightness blinds us so we look away. We hide from the truth by using unconscious defence mechanisms (as explained more precisely in my book *Stress Buster*). We often qualify our weaknesses by rationalising them, projecting them, displacing them, suppressing or repressing them etc. This has to stop. Looking at 'us' without the rose-tinted spectacles of Freudian defence mechanisms is not a pretty sight at times I have to tell you. But it is only when you accept the weaknesses of 'self' that you can exorcise them and build strength and integrity where weakness and frailty once reigned.

This takes a bundle of self-honesty and information. They say that we are what we know, well, we will need to know a lot about self-mechanics if we are to fix up our own faulty engines. My book *Stress Buster* is one step in the right direction; the rest will come from watching and studying ourselves and others. Experience is also a great teacher, especially when it incorporates a small war or two. Metaphorically engaging in small wars with the self is like immersing a bicycle inner tube into a bowl of water and applying air pressure to find out where the 'holes' are. The rising bubbles identify leakage, it is then down to us to get the repair kit out and mend. Invariably it is the self-leaks that stop us from completely achieving our life's goal and becoming higher echelon people.

Disquiet is all around us, but most of it is hidden beneath layers of consciousness so deep that we never have to look it right in the eye, or face the discomfort of dealing with it. The disquiet tends to come out in the forms of displaced pettiness, jealousy, envy, anger etc. This is why the tabloid press is so popular, and the negative TV soaps are high in the popularity polls, it is also why so many people love to sit around pulling others down, looking for the bad rather than the good in everyone. Let me tell you, once you are on this negative ride it is a downward spiral. It steals energy like a robber in the night. I try my best only to watch uplifting, inspirational or educational programmes. I limit my reading to the positive. If I am in company and the conversation becomes negative I'll either interject or turn the conversation to a more positive subject or leave the company. You'd be amazed how easy this is, also at how easily you can influence someone positively.

I remember sitting in a bar with Brian, many years ago. As we spoke a black guy walked past and Brian looked at me and said something about disliking 'niggers'. I hate that word, but it's the one he used. I was shocked because I'm normally a good judge of character and if I'd have thought for a second that this guy was prejudiced I wouldn't have been sharing my time with him. Anyway, he must have caught the look of disapproval in my face because he immediately tried to validate his dislike for black people. 'The only reason I don't like them Geoff,' he rationalised, 'is because they beat up their women.' I squinted my eyes as I tried to make sense of the drivel that Brian was coming out with.

'So what colour do you have to be to make beating up women OK?' I asked incredulously, 'I mean, I dislike anyone that hits women, what has colour got to do with it?'

'Well, yeah you're right Geoff,' he continued, 'I don't really mind coloured people. But you must admit, you wouldn't like it if your daughter brought one home.'

Bring one home? I shook my head in amazement. 'It doesn't matter to me in the slightest whether my daughters marry a white, red, yellow, black or purple man, as long as the bloke she marries treats her nice. What does colour have to do with it?'

He supped on his pint and looked sheepish. 'Yeah, suppose you're right really Geoff. It wouldn't matter. If my girl came home with a black guy I don't suppose I'd really mind.'

This young and silly man went, in the space of a few minutes, from being a raving KKK maniac to a lover of cultural diversity. And all because I didn't follow sheep-like in his line of talk.

If you can't change the conversation change the company and if you can't change the company change the environment.

The fact that we don't do anything about our problems automatically disqualifies, us from complaining about them. If we don't like it we should change it, if it can't be changed we should either live with it and stop moaning or move on. If we are not prepared to do anything about it we shouldn't bellyache about how cruel the world is.

My advice to all out there who want to get

on, is don't allow yourself to get pulled into what I call the 'soap syndrome'. This is where a group of people sit around the table gossiping about someone who isn't there, or slagging someone off that cannot defend themselves. This is the biggest waste of time and energy. I know it's hard, and it's very easy to get dragged into derogatory conversations, I've done it as many times as anyone else and I kick myself every time I fall into the trap, but if we want to achieve great things we have to start by making ourselves great, by making ourselves more pure and rise above the petty jealousies of everyday life. Re-train yourself to look for the good in each person and in each situation, fill your day with learning and speak only about the good that can be achieved.

I have a great friend John; I really admire him, especially for his restraint and tongue-control. One night a group of us talked about great martial artists and someone said to John, 'What about so-and-so, the guy that does Shotokan, is he any good?' John knew the man very well, he also knew that he was not a very reputable karate man, but rather than say that—it would have been very easy in the circumstances to say, 'Well actually I know him and he's not that good!'—John replied: 'So-and-so is not here to defend himself so I'd rather not talk about it.' It was brilliant, it changed the whole tone of the conversation and I really admired him for his strength to put a stop to the negativity. We should all aim so high.

If you are not used to it this can be really hard. I have actually lost a few of my old friends because of my reluctance to bad-talk others. Jane was always bitching about Tina, who was another friend of mine. Now it has to be said that not many people liked Tina, but I did, even though I could see why others didn't. She had done nothing to me but be a charming lady, but she had really upset Jane. Every time I was in company with Jane she would start to talk about Tina in a disparaging way, always concluding with, 'What do you think Geoff?' And I'd always answer by saying, 'Actually I think she's dead nice!' Killed the conversation like a blue joke at a nunnery. Unfortunately, or fortunately depending upon your point of view, I no longer get invited to Jane's.

Again, no higher moral ground is being taken here, I still to this day have to check myself to make sure that I don't end up in conversations that pull others to pieces. It can be so infectious and often you are in knee-deep before you even realise it. I make as many mistakes as the next man and what I tell you, I also constantly tell myself. As a rule of thumb always ask yourself, 'If so-and-so were sat next to me would I be saying the things I am saying?' If not put a gate on your mouth. Or even try this little trick—it always works for me—when you feel like saying something bad about another person, deliberately make yourself say something good instead. For example, I was speaking with Jimmy just last night, he said, 'Oh I saw so-and-so the other day. They reckon he's a bit of a horrible bloke, you know him Geoff, is he horrible?' The chap he was asking about was not one of my favourite people and I had recently had words with him over some incident or other. As soon as Jimmy asked the question I felt the negative words racing to my lips and I immediately put a plug on them and instead said, 'Actually I don't know him well enough to make a comment, but I do know a lot of people that think he's a good bloke.' Then I changed the conversation at the speed of a London traffic warden and we moved on to more inspiring banter.

When people ask me about others, trying to draw me into the soap syndrome, I make the habit of imagining a tape recorder sat by my side, and that every word I utter will be recorded and taken to the person I am talking about right after my comments. After imagining this I suddenly find myself saying either great things or nothing at all. Make it a habit to talk nice or to not talk at all. Be aware especially when you are a little low or tired or stressed. When your guard is down the rancorous demon rears its ugly mug and infiltrates a tired mind. It is also the time that others tempt us into their world of moan-and-groan. If we are not very careful we end up talking down when really we should be talking up. Don't have any of it, get mad and remind yourself that it's unfair and a waste of your time and energy to engage in gossip. And beware that you don't fall into compliment-packaged gossip. I've found myself falling into this trap on many occasions. It's when you want to slag someone off but try to hide it in a nice complimentary package: 'Oh yeah, that John, he's a lovely bloke, dead nice, but don't trust him with money. The other day he borrowed some cash off me and I never saw it again, but he's dead nice really, lovely bloke.'

Think of energy as currency, every time you use it for something that is not productive you are literally throwing money down the drain. Don't waste something that is so precious. Your minutes and hours are priceless, please don't abuse them.

We are creators so let's start creating a new us, so that we might be who we really know we can be. Start by being honest and choosing the right influences.

I believe it was Sir Henry Wotton who said that, 'Virtue is the roughest way, but proves at night a bed of down.'

The lobster
Of course virtue—or the practice thereof—can be very uncomfortable, but don't forget that

discomfort is a sign of growth. Remember the lobster? It's always shedding its shell so that it can grow and evolve; it can be an uncomfortable process and it can leave you open to prey but it is what we must do otherwise we will never move from where we are to where we want to be.

In theory this premise (being virtuous) should be an easy one to understand, after all, we know the difference between right and wrong—don't we? Unfortunately there are a lot of grey areas when talking about this sticky subject because our truth, our 'right and wrong', is governed by our knowledge, and if our knowledge is a little on the thin side then our truth—though we may be unaware of it— is usually wrong. So when we think we are doing right we are actually, and inadvertently, doing wrong. But don't panic. Being wrong is often one of the steps that we take on the way to being right. I said before that we are what we know, I'll add to that; we also believe what we know, in fact, our truth is determined by what we know and the more we know the more our truth changes and grows. That's why I think it's so imperative that we get a solid educational foundation, the more cultivated we can become the greater our truth can be. If you learn something new every day your world will change on a daily basis.

If you learn nothing you will always be living in the same dreary place facing the same dreary problems, probably blaming the world for your lot. Every time I look at people it is as though I am looking for the first time at a brand new world. The information I am gathering makes it so. If you have a profound understanding about sociology (the environment), psychology (the mind) and physiology (the workings of the human body), your whole perception of the world changes and you develop a great compassion for your fellow man. If I look at a car and an engine mechanic looks at a car do you think we both see the same thing? Of course not. I see a hunk of metal that takes me from A to B—and I'm not quite sure how it does it, only that it needs petrol and oil and the like on a regular basis. He sees a masterpiece of mechanical genius, he sees camshafts and pistons, horse-power, blah-de-blah. He sees a livelihood, something that puts food on the table for his kids, something that he knows every nut and bolt about. If it makes a clicking sound when the engine is running he'll know what it is, what new part it needs, where to get the part from, how much the part will cost with and without labour, how to fit it and even how many miles you'll be able to do before it'll need replacing. All I'll know is the phone number of the guy that'll charge me a fortune to fix it, and I'll have to look that up in my filofax. It is only information that makes this so, and if I get the same information I too can

106

change a hunk of moving metal into a vehicle of genius.

My only worry in life is that there are not enough hours in the day to get all the information that I would like. There are not enough days in the year to speak with all the great people I want to speak with; not enough years in my life to taste everything, see everything, hear everything. But I know one thing, even if I don't touch every corner of my world it won't be for the want of trying. I want my truth to change, I want to know more, but I know that at this moment in time my mind is not big enough to take it all in, but in time it will be. Isn't it incredible that we once believed the world was flat, and with the information we had at that time of course that was our truth. No one would have told us any different. And if they did we might have burned them at the stake, and justified our actions because that too would have been our truth. With more information we realised how silly a notion this flat-world theory was. As a nightclub doorman I used to hit people over the head if I felt they were a threat to me, but I felt fine about it because, at that time, I thought I was right, that violence was justifiable. With the information (very limited I'm afraid) that I had at the time, that was my truth. With the information I have now I can't believe how wrong I was and how much violence limited me and how others hated and were frightened of me. I can now see that I was not justified in the violence I enacted, and given my time again, with the information I now hold I'd have done it all differently. Even great men like Gandhi and Stephen Hawking and others throughout history have had to contradict themselves because increased knowledge has shown their old and true concepts to be old and untrue. Much of the war going on throughout the world now is being fought by two sides that both believe, categorically and without question, that they are right and their opposition wrong. Their growth to a newer truth is jammed by anger and fear and many deaths and personal losses will result before they are liberated and a new paradigm is born.

So truth is a very subjective matter and we must strive not only to allow our own truth to mature but also to allow others a different truth, and perhaps guide the less mature along a more productive path. We must understand that no one is really right or wrong, there are just different levels of truth.

Once you have a developed truth it enables you to see the things in life that are not productive, and thus avoid them. One of the best ways to gain more energy to help us on our journey is to actively resist what we know to be untrue and not allow ourselves to fall for the infantile defences that rationalise faulty behaviour.

Every time you resist the untrue you receive

the gift of empowering energy. But the opposite is also true; every time you fall into temptation, energy is taken away from you, it leaks like a faulty sump and you go one step back on your journey.

Freud felt that this 'energy gift' came from an infinite power supply at the very core of our subconscious and is given to us as a reward from the super ego, (a part of the consciousness called the internal parent) for doing good. Equally and oppositely, he felt, the super ego also punishes us with feelings of guilt and low self-worth, it takes away our empowering energy if we do wrong.

So every time we are tempted by the untrue, stealing, lying, judging others, cheating, infidelity, envy, greed, jealousy etc. but fight and resist that wrong, we get a gift of energy that can power our journey. If we use this energy to give to others in the form of love (helping others, doing good deeds etc.), it comes back to us tenfold. It says so in the Christian Bible, but if you don't follow the Christian doctrine then take my word for it, I make it work all the time.

The more fuel we have the easier it is to reach our goals. Like the car we need a source of fuel otherwise we end up on the roadside courting rust and shitty pigeons, so it pays to invest our energy into others at any and every given chance.

In a way that dark part of us, what Carl Jung called the 'shadow side' (he was another eminent psychologist, one of Freud's students), can be a climbing-frame to the stars because every time we resist and do the right thing we grow, we change our mind and climb to greater heights. So everything we need to get 'there' is in us, if only we can learn how to use the controls.

I have found that the higher we climb the greater the temptation we encounter. If you were a religious person you might look at this as a test from God. I don't think that God tests us to be honest. I don't think he sits up there saying, 'He's doing well let's test him, see if we can trip him up.' What do you think? Do you reckon God, 'unconditional love', the Christos, the great light of love, the force that moves planets and creates the universe is sitting up there playing with our lives? I don't think so. I think the temptations are greater because the game is bigger. But equally when we resist big temptations the rewards are big too, but if we give in to big temptations the consequences are often so big that they ruin us.

How many times have you seen people from all walks of life, that are at the top of their field, lose everything by giving in to the untrue? It's in the news every day. One of the things about growing into big fish is that you attract the serious angler who wants to tempt us out of the pond with tasty enticements that hide the hook that might finish us. Don't think of this as a bad thing. When we are small we attract small temptations that allow us to grow when we resist and to use them as a climbing-frame. Similarly when we get bigger we attract big temptations that will allow us to grow even bigger and subsequently help more people that might be further down the ladder.

A budding musician might attract a small following of female fans, perhaps he is married and one or two of the fans make a pass at him, not too big a temptation really. But when that same musician becomes a household name, he is probably going to be tempted by some of the most beautiful women in the world. Now, that would be a temptation for most people and if he wants to retain his integrity, keep his marriage and be true to himself then he'd better watch out. If he gives in to the temptation he risks possibly everything he holds dear.

So I see the temptations as being less like tests and more like fuel stops along the way because every time you 'resist', you fill up with fuel (a gift from the super ego). See them not so much as devilish temptations but more like angelic opportunities. When we resist the untrue we grow in esteem and empower our journey.

Be careful because the temptations can

often be hidden or vague and there will be plenty of people around trying to convince you to succumb, and that it is good to give in and that, 'Hey, everyone does it, it'll be OK.'

Every little thing needs to be in place, everything from not fiddling the taxman to treating everyone equally. The list goes on and often it can be a very difficult task sorting out what is right and what is wrong. If you inject self-honesty into the equation the truth usually rises to the top. I can't tell you what your truth is, only you know that, but I do know one thing, every time you get it wrong you lose energy and end up taking a retrograde step.

One of my great heroes in life is a wrestler and strong man called George Julius Hackenschmidt (I did say you'd be hearing a bit about this gentleman). I read his book *The Way to Live* printed in 1904 and learned a great lesson from this man mountain. He said that, 'One ought to avoid all unnecessary worry and exciting thoughts, and to cultivate a firm tranquillity of mind. Melancholy reflections will in no way influence fate, whereas one may weaken the constitution by the waste of energy while indulging in them.'

Now I don't want to sound like a killjoy here, but overexcitement does run away with our energy. Have you ever felt how exhausting it can be to get overexcited about something? When I was younger I actually used to make myself ill by getting overexcited before

Christmas and holidays. I used to sit and talk about it all the time, when I wasn't talking I'd be thinking, even dreaming about it. Then after the event I'd be physically and mentally low, sometimes actually clinically depressed. I didn't know it then though I realise now that all my energy was being wasted in anticipation of something that never seemed to live up to the picture that I had built in my mind. Even now I have to be careful about letting my excitement run away with me. I have a biological excitement for life that, if not controlled, leaves me emptier than a eunuch's Y-fronts. Excitement, stress, worry or anticipation all release similar hormones into the blood and arouse the body. It often forces the brain into overload and that very small organ, only two per cent of the overall body weight, will use up to 50 per cent of our oxygen supply. Small wonder that overexcitement has us exhausted before the anticipated event even unfolds.

A little bit is nice, it's lovely to look forward to things, just don't allow it to run away with all the fuel that you are going to need when the event arrives. It's a bit like sitting at the lights in your car with the gears in neutral and the foot full on the accelerator waiting for the lights to change.

We also have a problem with leaks in this worrisome decade. We can be full of fuel and raring to go, but if there are leaks in the boat then it is only a matter of time before we sink. We need to locate these leaks and seal up the hole or we are going to be forever moving one step forward and two steps back. Chuang Tse (a great Chinese guy is all I know) said that, 'When the body is kept bustling about without stop, it becomes fatigued. When the mind is overworked without stop, it becomes worried, and worry causes exhaustion. The nature of water is that it becomes clear when left alone and becomes still when undisturbed. It is the symbol of heavenly virtue.'

He was right of course and worrying too much about things doesn't help either, this too will click the brain into '50 per cent mode' and gobble up the petrol like a greedy engine. If it is within your power to change something that worries you, then change it as soon as possible, get the monkey off your back before it starts getting fat. If it is outside your circle of influence, that is, it is not within your power to change, then don't even spend a single second thinking about it. Deal with it or live with it. Sounds easy when you say it I know, but it can be very difficult to just stop worrying. So practise. That's how we change ourselves and become bigger.

Treat it like a session down the gym and work out, use your worries as sparring partners, practise abstaining from worry. Strip the worry to its bare essence and lay it out on the table. What is it that really worries you?

What is the worst thing that can happen if your greatest worry should actually occur? Tell yourself that should 'it' happen you'd handle it, you'd deal with it. Then set about making the worst case scenario better. Just keep talking to yourself in your mind and telling yourself that you can handle it, you can deal with it. Keep your thoughts positive at all times, when the negative thoughts come into your mind imagine that they are little tennis balls and bat them back out again. When the thoughts start sneaking in the back door, open it and laugh at them, tell them that they have been caught and then bat them back out again. If they come in a hundred times knock them back out a hundred and one times. Sometimes it can be a real battle but remember the battle will make you strong. If you don't fight then the thoughts will rape and pillage. Have a fight and keep having a fight. If you find that the negative thoughts have got through and you are infused with feelings of anxiety, take a minute and examine the feelings. Breathe very deeply through your nose, calm yourself and examine what it is that you are so frightened of. Don't think about what has caused the feelings or the consequence of the feelings, just feel them. Talk to them, thank them for coming in, and invite them in greater quantities. The way to rid yourself of these feelings is to be at one with them. It takes a bit of bottle, believe me I know, I've been there enough times, but it does work if you don't panic and talk very positively to yourself and keep talking positively to yourself until the self-instruction becomes a daily habit.

Always try to do the very best that you can then leave the rest up to She-who-looks-over-us.

Great strength also comes from prayer and from meditation, though I suspect that they are probably one and the same, as much from the respite they offer as anything else. As I have already said, it is important that we work hard but the work needs to be intermittent, that is, we also need to rest hard and to play hard too. Rest falls into the sleep category and play falls into the meditation category because when we focus on play it takes our mind off the things that stress us out and allows the brain to rest.

Prayer and meditation allow us to focus the brain on a mantra and give it much needed rest; prayer and meditation performed correctly, are possibly better for us than actual sleep because the brain goes deeper into the unconscious during these periods. It allows the mind to recharge its batteries and also allows us to pick up energy from all that is around us.

Rule Seven

You need a goal to shoot at

Sitting in the Stardust Hotel with one of my lifetime heroes, Mr Chuck Norris, I asked him what was the important thing about achieving your dreams. As a man who has achieved all of his own lifetime goals I thought he'd be the right chap to ask. He said, 'Setting a goal, getting a visual image of what it is you want is very important. You've got to see what it is you want to achieve before you can pursue it. I've always found that anything worth achieving will always have obstacles in the way. You've got to have that drive and determination to overcome those obstacles en route to whatever it is that you want to accomplish. A lot of people give up just before they're about to make it. You never know when that next obstacle is going to be the last one. A lot of times people give up and say, "Well, I can't do it," but that next obstacle might have been the final one for them. So I always kept that in my mind and I'd say to myself, "Well maybe the next one, the next person I meet might be the one." You need the tenacity to stick to it when things get tough and have faith that you can do it.'

Rule Seven is: *'You need a goal to shoot at.'*

Otherwise you're not playing football, you're just kicking a ball aimlessly around the park.

It helps to have a goal. In fact, if you haven't got a goal it's pretty difficult to succeed because you don't know what it is you want to succeed in. Even with all the energy in the world goals that aren't specific are rarely attained. When you really set your heart and soul on an idea, on a goal—and I really mean every single part of you pointing in the same direction—it's almost impossible for it not to happen. It's almost as though, once you have set your mind to it the whole universe conspires to make it so. So far in my life I have achieved everything that I have completely committed myself to. The things that didn't happen I didn't want enough, and now, looking back, I can see very clearly that I didn't totally want it, even if at the time I thought I did. I do the job I want for a living and work for myself, my wife is my dream girl, my kids are beautiful, I have great friends, I mean proper friends that love me, and me them, my house is gorgeous and I am in a position to drive whatever car I want, and I do. I don't mean this to sound conceited or big-headed, just to say that I only write about what I know, the things you are reading are not theories that I think you might like to hear or ideas that'll give you a bit of a boost. They are true, they are actual, I am living proof that they work, that you can have whatever you want—if you set your heart on it, if you really want it and are prepared to make getting these things your life, and not just a fad for the next few days.

I have a friend, Len Dusaquid (for want of a better alias), who has a million ideas. He has so many ideas that he is falling over them but he has not managed to bring any of them to fruition because his ideas rarely get beyond the note-pad. And some of his notions are brilliant; when he tells me about them I think, 'Yeah, that's a great idea.' One or two of the ideas I've actually thought, 'Wow! I wish I'd thought that up.' My friend is one of the most talented, the nicest, most gentle . . . and unfulfilled men you could ever wish to meet. I was with him recently and he is onto more new ideas. Unfortunately, other people completely unrelated to him have brought some of his better ideas, the ones he didn't follow through, to fruition; other people that have had the same idea and gone on to make their fortune with it. I was the very same as a young man writing sketches for TV that I did nothing with, only to watch helplessly as a couple of years later the same ideas appeared on my TV screen as finished products because someone else had beaten me to it. Ideas and goals are like seeds in a sack that do nothing but gather dust and go off if they are not planted into fertile ground. How many seeds do you have planted right now? Some of my martial arts friends are brilliant at their art, some of them champions, and yet, even with all their hard-earned skills, they still haven't got two pennies to rub together, they still aren't fulfilled. One of these chaps came to have a chat with me. He was a world champion in karate—in the amateurs where there is no pay—he'd trained for twenty-five years and yet he still had to make his living, a meagre one at that, in a factory. He felt life had dealt him a bad hand and that, as a champion, the world should be knocking at his door to offer him a living. If he was a footballer that might be the case, football is a very popular sport, perhaps the most popular. As a martial artist, however, you can be world champion and still a complete unknown outside of the martial arts. Also, he was facing the fact that, in the martial arts, there are a lot of world champions in different styles, so many in fact that often—unfairly I think—they can even be unknown within their own specialist field. He wanted to know what he was doing wrong and why he was still having to get up to his neck in grease and oil fifty hours a week, when lesser martial artists, often people that couldn't fight the tide in the bath, were 'raking it in' to quote my friend. I asked him how many seeds he had planted. He looked at me like I had three heads. 'I'm world champion!' he said incredulously.

'Yeah,' I replied, 'being the world champion is your bag of seeds, and a big bag too but how many of those seeds have you actually planted? How many people outside the martial arts, or even within the martial arts actually know that you are a world champion? What have you actually, physically, done to sell what you have?' I explained that the 'lesser martial artists' he despised so much should be the ones he looked to for inspiration because their small bag of seeds had made them financially secure and fulfilled because they had planted and tended to every single one. And they'd had the wisdom to plant them in very fertile ground. I told him that he shouldn't despise them just because they had achieved what he couldn't, he should admire them for their ingenuity. I find these lovely people awe-inspiring because they show us all that you don't have to be the most talented person in the world, you just have to plant and tend to every seed in your possession.

When I came away from being a bouncer to work as a full-time martial artist I was not a great karate man, I was no world champion, just a good club player. I was never brilliant though my work ethic was always prolific. People—now that I am well known—seem to think that I was a world class martial artist and my success inevitable. At that time I was an unknown away from the nightclub door and even then completely unknown outside of Coventry. But I had a couple of important seeds to plant and plant them I did. I stole a world niche in my art, not because I was great or the best but because I was first and I planted what I had well, I planted like a man possessed, I planted like there was no tomorrow. There were many other people on the scene far better and more able to take the niche than me, they had so many seeds they were beyond counting. But they didn't plant them, not a single one, and me with only a very small bag of seeds; I planted the whole jolly lot. Later of course, because I reaped the harvest of those seeds, I had many more to plant. Time allowed me to nurture more seeds by training with the very best people in the world, until I went from a club player to the world stage, eventually being invited to teach for Chuck Norris in Las Vegas, Nevada. I know that people will say, 'I used to train with Geoff Thompson, I was much better than him,' and maybe they were, but they are still turning a lathe, up to their nuts in oil and grease and I am sitting pretty enjoying every moment of my life. I may not have had as many seeds as them but my goodness, I did plant every single one. I also learned new skills and eventually took my talents to the bigger circus. I started planting mainstream seeds: writing for health magazines; writing for television, cinema and stage; appearing on radio and TV and generally becoming a legend in my own boxer shorts.

Napoleon Hill advised us that, 'If one does

his work in harmony with nature's laws, and performs the necessary amount of labour, nature takes over the job where the farmer's (the planter of seeds) labour ends, germinates the seed he plants and develops it into a crop of food. And,' he continues, 'observe thoughtfully this significant fact: for every grain of wheat or corn he plants in the soil, nature yields him a hundred grains, thus enabling him to benefit by the law of increasing returns.'

So set your goal in your sights and then start planting seeds to make it happen. Make sure that you plant the seeds believing 100 per cent that they will grow. HAVE FAITH. Thoughts, goals, dreams that are backed by faith always take precedence over all others in the matter of the definiteness and the speed with which they are handed over to the subconscious section of the mind and are always acted upon. Once the goal is firmly fixed in the subconscious and infused by faith, it sets to work to make it happen. Similarly Maxwell Maltz said goals and dreams implanted in the subconscious—to be really effective—must be accompanied by deep feeling and desire. He also said that we should picture to ourselves what we would like to be and have, and assume for the moment that such things are possible. Arouse a deep desire for these things. Become enthusiastic about them. Dwell upon them—and keep going over them in your mind. Your present negative beliefs were formed by passionate or fearful thought. Generate, therefore, enough emotion, or deep feeling, and your new thoughts and ideas will cancel them out and make it possible to plant thoughts of great things.

If there is any doubt in your mind as to whether or not you really want to achieve your goal you are unlikely to succeed. What I do to make my intention concrete is write it down on a note-pad. I write down what it is I intend to achieve and the time in which I intend to achieve it. Some people say they want something, but do they really? Deep down in their mind many do not commit themselves to their goals and dreams. So write it down, set a time limit and don't hesitate to tell people when they ask what you are going to do, talk and act as though it had already come to fruition. Eliminate all doubt from your mind.

It's no good having a million ideas and not setting definite sights on any one of them. Blunderbussing lacks focus and focus is what makes a goal sprout legs and come to life. The security man who wanted to be a singer is a good example of this. When I first spoke to him he said what a great singer he was, how he brought the house down every time he hit the 'open mic' and how his mates had told him he was 'better than that crap on *Top of the Pops*'. But when I told him I felt he hadn't planted enough seeds he suddenly started saying things like, 'Of course, what I'd really like to do is be a footballer, the manager at the city said . . .' or, 'See, my real dream is bodyguarding. My mum reckons . . .' Blah-de-blah. You get the picture. He didn't really know what he wanted to do. You can have anything you want but you can't have everything so choose and then take it. Commit yourself completely or don't bother at all. Throw everything you have at it, or stay at home. I think it was Emerson that said great men are those that know thoughts rule the world. So make your thoughts big, then plant them with desire and faith. Set your sights, aim and fire. Make it so.

Changing direction
One of my friends said to me, 'I really want to become a lawyer, but it's a five-year course, what if I get half-way through the course and change my mind?'

I told him that nothing is cast in stone. If you are half-way towards your goal and suddenly realise that you are on the wrong path you can change to another. It's allowed, it's all allowed. And don't feel as though what you have done thus far will be wasted, it won't. Any knowledge you learn en route can be used and re-used in different directions. Even if it isn't specific to your next goal it will matter not. When we acquire knowledge, when we stretch our mind to take in new information our consciousness becomes broader, we become more erudite, we become stronger and wiser. That strength and wisdom can be applied to anything in life. It's like hitting the weights and building skeletal muscle and strength. Just because you have developed it pushing weights doesn't mean that you can't apply that same strength and muscle into other areas. Of course you can.

This doesn't mean either that you can't aim for more than one goal at once. Though to aim in several directions at the one time does take a lot of skill and energy, but it can be done. I often aim for several goals at once. To do this you have to become a juggler who manages to keep several balls in the air at once. This takes a great work ethic and time management. What I do, like the juggler, is only concentrate on each ball as it touches my hand, then it's back in the air again. Then I concentrate on the next. As a for instance, at this moment in time I am juggling several different balls. I write for three magazines, I am working with a theatre company on my plays, a film company on my serials and my films, I'm writing this book at 6 a.m., I'm just getting ready to start a book-signing tour of Britain, I am negotiating with several book clubs to sell my other books, I am dealing on a weekly basis with the reps who sell my books to the shops—do you get the picture? There's loads more too, and I know it can all sound daunting but I have built up to this over a long period of time. When I first started in this game I struggled to hold more than one idea in my head at one time. Any more and smoke started to come out of my ears. My mind was quite weak, but by placing it under pressure, by gently stretching it I changed it. Now it's strong. Over the years I have gradually learned to add more and more to my plate and still manage. But I still only really carry one in my head at any one time. All the rest are written down on my things-to-do board. I find that if I write down the jobs that aren't immediately necessary I don't have to think about them. If the phone rings and another job rears its head I'll write it on my to-do board and deal with it as soon as possible. Yesterday I was writing and my printers delivered several thousand books that had to be offloaded and placed into storage. So I stopped the writing and offloaded. It gave my head a rest from the computer and enabled me to complete another job. If I find that I have a deadline for a book or an article then I'll temporarily postpone all other jobs until the urgent one has been put to bed. If you do find that you are doing too much—because let's not forget that we also need time for rest and play—and the workload is getting too fat to carry, then drop a couple of the tasks, temporarily or permanently, until the schedule has slimmed down a little. Remember it's your time, your life, you just hire it out to projects and goals. If you find that you do not have enough time left for you or the family, then stop hiring it out.

Commitment to the goal is very important. Many times I have found myself half-committed and unsure. This is a sign that your aim will fall well short of your desires. If you are not sure, better not to start until you are. Or lay the facts out on the table and take a cold hard look at them. Strip away all the fears and emotions that may be attached and look at what is left. If it still looks beautiful then do it, if not or you're still not sure, write it down in your pending book until you are sure. When you do make the full commitment it'll happen, some times so fast that it scares the Y-fronts off you. A couple of years ago I reached a crossroads in my life where I had my feet in two different worlds. The world of teaching and the world of mainstream writing. And for a long time I tried to do both, never quite committing myself totally to either. On the one hand I wanted to write mainstream so that I could stretch my abilities. But that meant starting at the bottom again and working myself up. Very uncomfortable but vital if you want to grow. On the other hand I was comfortable in the teaching, I was in demand on the seminar circuit and the martial arts books—though they were no longer stretching me—were easy to do because I had written so many. Going into the new world would be risky because I was the new guy and my living was no longer guaranteed, whereas in the teaching circuits I had carved myself a solid niche. I knew one thing, I couldn't continue to do both because the load was starting to weigh me down. When I laid the facts out on the table I could clearly see that although the seminars were paying me a good wage and they were regular, my heart was no longer in them. I felt I'd said all I wanted to say. The books and videos I had produced on martial arts were selling as well as ever but I had no inclination to write and produce any more, similarly I had said all I wanted to say and didn't want to tear the bottom out of it. Whereas with the mainstream writing I felt a real passion, an urgency to get in there and make my mark, I *wanted* to be in an arena where I was the least known, the bottom of the pack, I wanted to be with people that could help develop my skills and take them to the next level. The only thing stopping me was my old friend fear (for more on fear please refer to my books *Fear—The Friend of Exceptional People* and *Stress Buster*), and a bit of laziness too. I was comfortable where I was and I knew that my place was pretty secure. Mainstream writing meant being out there fronting failure again, fighting against the unknown. I made my decision to drop the courses and head for the bigger circus. I set a date and told everyone that asked, and a few that didn't, what my intentions were. My last course was

129

set for the December that year. I even wrote it down. On the course I told all present of my intentions, this made the commitment final. It was a great course and a great weekend in London, and a great feeling to have finally made my decision. When I arrived home from London on the Sunday evening there was a message on my answer machine from one of the major men's magazines in London offering me my own column. I was delighted. As I said, once you commit yourself the whole universe conspires to make it happen. You will meet all the right people and serendipity (unexpected coincidences) will become a normal part of your everyday life. But it doesn't happen until you make a decision and choose a direction. Remember, if you don't have a goal you're not playing football; you're just kicking a ball around the park.

Rule Eight

It's tenacity that determines capacity

One thing I have learned and one thing I know is that providence will rarely knock at your door, but if you go out into the street it *will* meet you half-way.

I was on the radio once, Radio 4, being interviewed by a very lovely man called Tom Robinson. I complained to Tom that I didn't have an agent and, at the time, I felt I could do with one. He asked me how many I had been in touch with. I said something like, 'Oh loads.' I'd probably rung about a dozen in a mad spurt one day and then never tried again. Some of the people I'd rung were kind but unhelpful, some were downright rude and couldn't get me off the phone quick enough. I told Tom about this in a kind of 'feeling sorry for myself' type of way. He gave me a piece of advice that I have quoted many times since that day. He said that if there were fifty agents in London and I had only rung forty-nine then I hadn't done my job. If I had rung all fifty, but only once then I still hadn't done my job because on the second time around the chances are I'd be talking to completely different people, or even the very same people on a better day. 'If you want an agent,' he told me kindly but emphatically, 'you'll find an agent.' I can see now that my time was invested more in feeling hard done by than it was in tenaciously tracking down a great agent and making him take me on, I learned Rule Eight from Mr Robinson: *'It's tenacity that determines capacity.'*

At this moment in time I have twenty-something books published and over a quarter of a million copies in print, but that didn't just happen overnight, it started really small, with just one book published and a couple of thousand sold.

These kinds of sales didn't just materialise out of thin air. There were many refusals en route, many setbacks, numerous times when I doubted my abilities, many lonely and sad hours reading and re-reading refusal letters for some sign of encouragement.

It wasn't just talent that got me from the note-pad to the bookshop, it was tenacity. Let me tell you my story, how I got my first book on the shelves.

I can't tell you how hard it is to receive the standard refusal letter from a publisher and then have to send the same manuscript out the same day to another. After you get a few of these you really do start to wonder if it will ever change. Many people think that you just arrive, they think, 'Oh it's all right for you, you're published.' But I wasn't always published; I didn't always have dozens of books on the shelf at WH Smith and Waterstone's. There was a journey, and it was a very hard journey.

For me it all started with one book *Watch My Back*, published by a then very small publisher. I wrote the book in the toilet of a local factory that hired my time to herd their dust, I swept floors. I was a 'dust cowboy'. And I was stone-broke. I was living with a lady that absolutely hated the very thought of me being a writer, and she scared the shit out of me so I had to write my book in secret. I had no qualifications; I left school with nothing but my good looks and directions to the nearest factory looking for lathe-turners and bog-cleaners. I had absolutely no idea about writing books, where to start, how to set it out, who to send it to when and if I ever got the thing finished, I didn't even have enough cash to have the book typed out. All I had was a good story and ignorance. If I had thought about all the things that were against me I probably would never have written my name at the top of the first page. As it was I had a mate at work on the machines (hi Steve) who thought I could do it and that was enough to get me started. So I went to the stores and got myself a note-pad and a pen—I told them I needed to do an inventory for the dust I'd been sweeping as loads had been stolen—and started to work. I couldn't really write at home because, as I said, it would have caused me a lot of marital grief and I was more frightened of her than I was of the foreman, she was bigger than him for one thing. So I hid myself away in the toilets and started to write. The first day I ended up with half a pad full of words, a permanent red ring around my bum and numbness in my lower limbs. I got off the loo, pleased with my day's work, and promptly fell over. I couldn't get back up again until the feeling returned to my legs. It wasn't long before I had run out of paper and so it was back to the stores again for more. In the end I filled four pads and finished the first draft of my first book.

How many excuses do you think I could have found not to write my book? There were a million reasons I could have used to back out from the task. The environment was a shit one for writing (if you'll forgive the pun) but I made it the right environment by improvising. Actually, writing the book wasn't the hardest part; it was hiding from the foreman. I disappeared into that toilet for weeks.

Once the book was written I kept it in a cupboard at home, not really knowing where to go from there. I mean, where do you go, what do you do with a book written in longhand on lined note-pads? I was a dust herdsman in the factory; I didn't have a clue about publishing.

See, when you're at school they don't really prepare you for this kind of thing. If you want to be a writer or a tobogganist, they don't have a clue what to do with you. They're more tuned in to preparing you for 'proper jobs'. Instructions on how to get a bus from the comprehensive to the local factory were more common than how to get a book published. I didn't know anyone who wrote books—who do you speak to? I decided to go to the local newspaper, the *Coventry Evening Telegraph,* and ask their advice. I met a lovely reporter called Sue Larey. 'How do I get this published?' I said, handing her a dog-eared copy of *Watch My Back*. She was very kind. She could quite easily have fobbed me off with the obligatory 'I'm dead busy' but she didn't. She read my book and helped me so much. In retrospect I can see that I probably put her on the spot because I just turned up unsolicited with a very raw typescript and said, 'Read that will ya?' But she agreed to look at it and give me an honest critique—I only hoped that the advice didn't include the words 'crap' and 'get a real job'. The first thing she said, even before she read it, was how well I'd done to actually write a book. She said that every newspaper office in the country was filled with reporters who all wanted to write books but who'd not managed to do so. That, she said, already put me ahead of the crowd. After reading the book she said she liked it, though looking back I'm not sure she was completely convinced because it was still very raw at that time. Her advice was to make the book longer and add more description. She felt that where I had used description it was strong and original. It had brought a smile to her face. If I could add more throughout the book it would stand a better chance of avoiding a publisher's dustbin.

I thanked her effusively and made off to extend my book.

She also recommended that I acquire a copy of *The Writer's Yearbook*, which would tell me all I needed to know about getting into print. I bought the book and started sending very poorly presented manuscripts with badly spelt letters to prospective publishers. In one letter I actually apologised for the 'atrocious spelling', ironically 'atrocious' was just about the only word in the letter I spelt right. Of course *The Writer's Yearbook* didn't advise this, they didn't have a section on 'how to send in badly presented work' rather the opposite in fact, but I didn't read it all, I just looked at the bits I liked and then posted off my work. I was in a hurry; patience was still a virtue I had not developed. Some of the prospective publishers I sent my parcel to must have had a right shock when they opened the package and this bundle of ill prepared pages fell out knocking coffee cups off tables and scaring the shit out of delicate commissioning editors. I bet some of the more sensitive publishers handed it over to the police and begged for twenty-four hour protection. I'm exaggerating of course, but it was in a right state when I sent it off.

Not surprisingly I had nothing back from the publishers but standard refusal letters and 'Don't call us we'll call you' type rebuttals. The more polite of the bunch said, 'Thanks but no thanks.' Others, obviously offended by my work, cut right to the chase and said, 'Leave your number in the bin.' It was pretty disheartening.

The refusal letters were coming in thick and fast. At one point I was actually getting more refusals in than I was sending manuscripts out, which was a little worrying. It was as though publishers were sending pre-emptive refusals just in case I sent my work to them. The word was obviously out and frightened publishing houses everywhere attacked first: 'No thank you Mr Thompson!' 'But I haven't even sent the book yet!'

I was getting more and more disheartened. In the end, I have to admit, I threw the manuscript in the bin vowing to never send it out again. Sharon, beautiful little thing that she is, fished it back out and insisted I keep sending it until someone said 'yes'. Which she was sure they would. She had believed in the book right from the very start and wasn't prepared to let it go without a hell of a scrap. So off it went *again* . . . and back it came *again*. Each time it came in we put it in an envelope and sent it back out.

After many refusals I decided that, before I sent it out again I was going to ring the publishers to see if they were actually interested in the premise before I wrapped my life in manila and sent it off to the raping fingers of some literary monster. Summersdale Publishers were one of the many names in the then 'Small Publishers' section of the Yearbook. I rang up and spoke to one of the partners, Stewart. I told him the premise of my book. Three hours later—if you have ever spoken with me on the phone you'll know exactly what I'm talking about—I asked if he was interested. He said he was, in theory, but would obviously have to see the book. So off it went.

I was back to letterbox-waiting and disappointments when the postman passed me by.

Periodically, while I awaited the reply, I read over the manuscript and, according to the mood I found myself in, would both like and loathe my work. Some days I'd read a chapter and think, 'Yeah, this is good.' Then other days I would read the very same pages and hate every word and wonder why on earth I ever thought I could get it published. Even after I received my first cheque for a film script, many years later, there were, and are, still days of doubt that have to be removed before I can get my fingers a-tapping on the keyboard. I've come to the conclusion that these feelings are a part of being a writer, this offers little solace, so when the self-doubt comes through the door, I kick its arse out of the window.

A couple of weeks went by. By day I was in the factory, telling stories, hiding from the foreman and occasionally pushing the brush. At the weekends I still worked the doors. The waiting—a part of the job, I'd been told—was corrosive. Every morning I listened for the heavy clump of Royal Mail boots on my doorstep. Then one sunny morning, ironically the very first day I wasn't up and at the door waiting for the postman like an obedient Labrador hungry for some finger snacks, it arrived. I heard the familiar plop of post on mat and rushed down the stairs, nearly tripping over my feet, in a race with excitement. There was no parcel; that was the first good news. It was a good start. Parcels—

as far as writers sending manuscripts are concerned—are a metaphoric boot in the bollocks. An early morning package with the immortal word 'No!' hidden somewhere beneath a very impersonal rebuttal are enough to kill the day deader than Darwin, often even the week, and for some of the more sensitive writers out there, a whole career. Parcels from publishers simply do not muck about; there is no preamble, no blue letter then red-letter building you up to the inevitable KO. No consideration for the writer's esteem just Bang! Right in the spuds. 'You can sod off because you're not good enough.' 'No!' That's what it says. It's so final. Don't you think? Final. It is so absolute. And such a shock too. You send your life off in manila and think, 'Maybe this is the one.' Then it comes back, sometimes after months and months and all it says is no! You'd think they might build you up to it a little, pyramid the refusal in some way, layer the refusal, perhaps start the letter off with a polite, 'Listen, we know you're trying really hard, and some of your stuff's not at all bad but "no".' Small case and in brackets please. It would definitely help.

Parcels? They mean that the publishers have sent your manuscript back and it is enclosed, often in the very envelope that you sent it in, sometimes they even pop in a bill for the postage and even more often unread, you can tell, believe me. But letters, now then, that

140

is a horse of a very different colour. Letters say, yes, yes or maybe! When you get a letter the day is suddenly grand and the world a lovely place in which to live and your knackers are safe for another day. Normally a letter means that you are at least in with a fighting chance.

I quickly scrambled through the day's post and bang! There it was. A letter from Summersdale.

I rushed to open my letter but then stopped in trepidation. Actually it was closer to unadulterated fear. Holding my spuds with one hand just in case and the letter in the other I hesitated; and then rushed to the loo where I sat and opened the letter, praying that the literary equivalent of 'get a proper job you spanner' was not emblazoned across the front of the page like an epitaph to the death of 'another submission'.

Ironically I was reading the acceptance for my first book in the very same place that I wrote it, on a toilet. A bouncer getting a book published! Even I was surprised.

I read very quickly that Summersdale had liked the manuscript, actually I only sent sample chapters and they wanted to see more. Could I supply them with further chapters? Could I ever Trevor! I nearly woke the whole neighbourhood when I ran back upstairs to tell Shaz the good news. Sharon was over the moon and after a celebration breakfast—I was

141

a writer now, I had to celebrate—a stark realisation set in. I couldn't send the rest of the book because I still hadn't finished the changes that Sue Larey suggested I make.

So over the next week I borrowed two typewriters—that made three with the one that I had already—and between me, Sharon and Alan, my brother-in-law, we finished the book—me writing the original by hand and them typing, in two different typefaces, what I had written. We worked until midnight every night to get the book finished and only stopped for the odd curry and bottle of wine. Eventually we finished the job and sent what we thought was a lovely job off to the publishers. We were pretty pleased with ourselves. Having written with three different typewriters and on two different paper shades it was closer to the Quasimodo of typescripts than it was to a 'good job'. The lads at Summersdale must have wondered what they'd let themselves in for when this offensive package landed on their doorstep. Irrespective of the mish-mash that I sent in they—Stewart and Alastair—liked what they read and had the great insight to see past the presentation. Within a couple of weeks they made me an offer to publish the book.

That's how it started for me, I wasn't headhunted, I didn't get the fairy-tale offer with a big up-front royalty cheque, I got refused about a hundred times more than I got accepted. It was only once the ball was rolling that other doors started to open for me.

Jimmy, one of my mates who was trying to break into the seminar scene (him trying to break in and me trying to break out! Who can figure?), also struggled to get his first start and complained to me that no one would sign him up for a seminar; he'd had enquiries but no firm bookings. This had happened even though he had given out several business cards. He said it in a kind of 'Well, I gave them their chance to have me and I'm not going to keep trying' way that hinted at snobbery. I know because I had been the very same myself when I first started. I went on to explain the number of times I had been turned down, let down, talked down and shoved out before I managed to make my name—and I am still working on it today. Even though I am known in one field, I only have to step into the next field and I am an unknown and have to start the process—from the bottom—all over again. After you've done it once of course it does get easier, there is a formula (keep knocking until someone answers) and it is the same wherever you go. I explained that he needed to get himself a profile in the magazines—which he had an open door to—so that every time people turn a page his mug is on display. He needed, I advised, to give the same people the same card again and again and again until they get him down for a course, even if it is just to stop him from giving them business cards. He also needs to be at every competition, seminar, martial arts meeting, or coffee morning meeting people, getting noticed and spreading the word. He needs to be at every show giving out cards and introducing himself, perhaps he could even offer his services free to a couple of people just to get his name about. When Chris Evans first got into local radio he worked for nothing just to get his foot in the door. He did it for nothing! Now he is worth a staggering 85 million.

I told my friend that he needs to have so many seeds planted that failure becomes an impossibility. Every minute of his day should to be invested in making it happen, making it so. Looking at it like this how can you fail? Tell me how can you possibly fail?

I remember when I got my first book, *Watch My Back* published by Summersdale. I was so inspired that I rang every TV show, radio station, newspaper, magazine and local *What's On* magazine to get the book promoted. I rang and rang and rang until my little dialling finger nearly fell off. And I managed to get on dozens of radio shows and about the same amount of TV talk-shows. I was actually sat in the green room of some of the best talk-shows on international TV with Hollywood stars. An agent on one such TV show looked at me across the green room like I was a martian and asked incredulously, 'How the hell did you manage to get onto this show? No offence, but it is usually restricted to major stars!' and I was hardly that, I was just a bouncer from Coventry who had written a book. I told him the truth. I just kept ringing until they had me on. I never took no for an answer. I was even on *Sky News,* live in front of something like twenty million people. It took me about six months to secure that deal, in the end I knew the researchers so well that they invited me to their Christmas party. The researchers said that they admired my tenacity and wanted to give me a shot. And they did.

Similarly, my friend Steve Jandu (Judo-Jandu) finished his bodyguard training with about thirty other lads all keen to break into the bodyguard field. How many of the thirty do you think secured work? One. Steve. And that's because he was the only one who didn't think his hard earned qualification was a licence to print money. All the rest thought that just because they had finished the course, the phone would be ringing off the hook and the offer letters would be making holes in the doormat. They never worked because they sat at home and waited for it to come to them. Steve realised that his qualification was not a licence to print money, rather it was a big bag of seeds that needed planting. That's where the money and the success would come, in the planting and not in the having of seeds. And plant he did. He sent out so many CVs and spoke to so many different people and ended up on so many different waiting lists that eventually he was turning work down. He had too much work—if there is any such creature. Tenacity is the one thing that bridges the gap between those that want and those that have. If you want a crop, plant your seeds, and the more seeds you have, the more crops you'll get, and the more crops you get the more seeds it brings.

The following are some case histories taken from my friend's book *Help—I Want To Work for Myself*. These are all people that knew where they were going and went there irrespective of the people that said they shouldn't or wouldn't or couldn't. They had seeds and tenacity.

There is much to be learnt from the examples of those who have found honest and original ways to build successful businesses. This is true in all areas of life: we learn from those who went before us, in order to avoid making the same mistakes. The world is too complex and ever changing for all conceivable lessons to have been learnt and recorded for posterity, so instinct, tenacity, common sense and inspiration will always be vital tools for a business-person. However, many of the experiences of the world's millionaires can nevertheless be applied to individuals who wish to follow in their footsteps.

Self-confidence is a great business asset, but

so is humility. Don't think that you know it all, even if you do! Pride comes before a fall, but having the humility to learn from others can be a key to success.

The examples below are all of people who have displayed brilliance and originality in their business dealings. Their experiences represent valuable lessons in business life, and should be remembered by those wanting to succeed.

Richard Branson is a millionaire who has built many different businesses with phenomenal success. With little formal education or business training he has risen from using a public telephone booth as an office to owning, among other things, an airline. He has avoided some of traditional business conventions such as wearing a tie and has always approached business in his own charismatic way, while keeping costs very low and passing on those benefits to the consumer. He has looked at many different areas of business and found gaps in the market where he felt he could provide better products or services than the competitors: the markets for fizzy drinks, insurance, condoms and commercial radio and recorded music have all been shaken up and made more competitive under his influence. He has diversified his business interests widely, which protects against the possibility of a drop in demand in one area of commerce affecting his business as a whole, and he always sets out to be both better and cheaper than his competitors when launching a new product or service.

But this is perhaps only part of the secret of his success. His high personal profile has gained his company publicity that could not possibly be bought: his attempts at setting ballooning records in a balloon emblazoned with his Virgin logo gained him prime time international news coverage, with his logo clearly visible. He has also become something of a media personality and a household name, always coming across as a pleasant character, uncontroversial and presenting a good image for his business. Branson is unusual in that he is as famous as his company: his name and that of Virgin are intrinsically linked. Therefore any publicity for himself is publicity for his business, and such publicity is cheap and easy for him to acquire.

Anita Roddick, founder of the Body Shop, has achieved phenomenal worldwide success with her chain of high street shops selling own brand toiletries and body care products. Right from the start her shop and its products were uniquely identifiable: simple but effective labelling and packaging gave a clear corporate image, which were both literally and environmentally 'green'. The avoidance of wasteful packaging and the refusal to allow animal testing ensured that consumers could always purchase goods at The Body Shop with a clear conscience. Whether Anita Roddick's business was instrumental in bringing about the 'green revolution' in consumerism that began to take off in the late 1980s, or whether her shops thrived as a result of the trend, is hard to say. However, the link between environmental issues and The Body Shop is now a strong one. Like Richard Branson, Anita Roddick is a high profile company leader whose actions to help improve lives in the third world and to help the environment reflect well on her business. Building The Body Shop has not been without its difficulties, of course. In the early days, Anita Roddick found herself unable to get vital funding from the banks, and instead sold a substantial share of the business to a local businessman for £5,000. That man is now a multi-millionaire. From its difficult beginnings, The Body Shop has grown to such an extent that in some countries there is barely a household without a Body Shop product in the bathroom or the bedroom.

If a business has genuine potential, such as in this case, there will always be investment funding available from somewhere, even if the usual avenues of finance are closed to you. The Body Shop also demonstrates how what begins as an 'alternative' shop can become the establishment. Culture, fashion, and buying habits are not set in stone: they can change given the right products and marketing.

P. Shaw, the inventor of 'cat's eyes' in the roads, became a multi-millionaire because his idea was ingenious, yet simple, and was so universal in potential that it was used not just on one road but on roads throughout Britain and other countries. The idea of a light-reflective unit to mark the centre of a road was inherently flawed: any such device would soon become dirty and would cease to function. Employing cleaners to polish regularly all the country's cat's eyes would be enormously expensive. Also, lenses in the road would be vulnerable to damage from car wheels. The way in which this design was special was that it incorporated a self-cleaning mechanism that solved both problems at once. Each lens is spring mounted, and the casing contains a stiff brush. When the wheel of a car drives over a cat's eye, as happens daily, the lens is pushed down into the casing, thus avoiding damage, and is wiped by the brushes, popping up clean after the car has passed. After he patented his design in 1934 it earned him a royalty on every one of the millions of cat's eyes sold. His original idea was so strong and foolproof that he was able to live off the proceeds for the rest of his life. There are very few opportunities such as this: he invented something that people perhaps didn't realise they needed. You need a particularly lateral thinking brain to look at life from a different slant and see how it could be improved for everyone in some, as yet undiscovered, way. There will be more like him, no doubt.

Sir Clive Sinclair is an amazingly innovative and forward thinking inventor, who has been the brains behind many of the modern electrical products that we now take for granted: pocket calculators, digital watches, and pocket televisions for instance. He was also one of the pioneers of home microcomputers, and invented a couple of electric vehicles. The Sinclair story is a valuable lesson to would-be entrepreneurs, for he has earned millions on some projects and lost millions on others. One of his biggest disasters was the Sinclair C5, the electric vehicle that failed to revolutionise personal urban transport. The concept of a single seat vehicle with silent electric operation and exemption from needing a driving licence is fine in a sensible, utilitarian world, but in the real world there is such a thing as image. Sinclair's fine scientific brain gave little thought to the concerns of most ordinary people: will they look silly in this sensible vehicle? Unfortunately, people did look silly. They were so close to the ground that pedestrians looked down on them, and the steering bars were below the seat level, which, though ergonomically superior to a standard steering wheel, did not 'feel cool'. Attention paid to pure ergonomic and scientific practicalities, instead of marketing an

151

appealing image cost Sinclair millions.

If your fortune is going to be built on a new product of your own invention, the lesson to be learnt from Sinclair is to concentrate as much on the image and styling of the product as on its utility. Image rules the lives of many people, and there is much money to be earned from its exploitation. Association of your product with someone who personifies a particular image is a great way to do this. Hence manufacturers of sports clothing sponsor top athletes to wear their products, because it gives the right image. The television pictures of a not-very-cool-looking Sir Clive Sinclair riding around in a C5 probably signed that product's death warrant.

Bill Gates worked hard for his success as the millionaire head of Microsoft. He toiled ceaselessly throughout his school years and after to become a talented and innovative computer programmer, often working at his computer until he fell asleep at the desk, and then waking up hours later and carrying straight on with the programming. His company's success rocketed after a commission from IBM to write the DOS software for the IBM PC, the computer that was to become the industry standard. This meant that every IBM and compatible computer in the world needed Microsoft soft-ware to make it run. This was followed by Windows, a graphical user interface of the type that had been developed by other companies and was adapted for the IBM PC. Today, Windows is the standard interface for all modern PCs, thus ensuring that software specification worldwide conforms to this interface. At the time Microsoft went public, Bill Gates owned 11,222,000 shares in the company, slightly over forty-nine per cent. He became a 'cash' millionaire by selling just 80,000 of them, while his remaining shares were worth about $350 million.

Bill Gates' company was 'small fry' when it first dealt with IBM, but now it has such market control that IBM's own graphical operating system (OS2) can barely get a foothold in the market. Bill Gates has proved that a small firm should not be afraid of dealing with and competing with a larger, longer established firm. In the end, it is the consumers who make the choices, and if you give them what they want there is no reason why you cannot take on the competition and win. As a business, Microsoft is run on relatively informal, though hard working, principles. Staff are expected to put in long hours at the office, and legend has it that one of them passed Bill Gates in the car park late one evening and said,

'Hey Bill, I've just been at work for twelve hours!'

'Oh,' replied Bill. 'Only working part-time, are you?'

Rule Nine

Use your time

As I sit and write this chapter the time is fast approaching 6.30 a.m. and what a beautiful time of the day this is, it's gorgeous, if it was a lady I'd be on my knees at this very minute saying, 'Marry me you beauty before I die of disappointment!' My cup of tea is hot at my lips and the sun is just starting to rise in the distant sky and I thank God for another day. It doesn't get a lot better than this I have to tell you. I want to share with you why I get up so early in the morning, I have this bladder problem you see, and why it is usually nearly midnight before I close the pages to my book and my eyes to the world. I've discovered that if you want to succeed in life you have to (Rule Nine) *'Use your time.'*

Sleep is important, I know that, we all need sleep, and I'm no genius for working that baby out, but I don't need as much as I once needed. In the not too distant past I needed at least eight hours, maybe more, before the starting handle would even consider turning my tired mind and body into some sort of action. But this sleep thing has always bothered me somewhat because I've always felt that a lot of it is a waste. Of course I know

154

that it isn't, we need rest and we need sleep as much as we need food and water, but we don't need to stay in bed so long that potatoes start growing under us. I always felt that long hours in bed were simply wasted time, so I did something about it. As a part of my internal training to become an inner athlete, an internal strong man, I started getting up earlier in the morning so that I could have more time to do the things that I wanted to do. And at 6.30 in the morning it is so very quiet that it is easy to concentrate and get loads done. No disturbances: peace and quiet. There is not even the sound of distant motors in the background. I also have a lovely feeling of excitement in my stomach because I feel, I know, that I am stealing time that would normally be lost to the bad habit of 'lying in'. I get two or three hours, every day, more than nearly everyone else. At the end of the night I sit in bed and read or study until my eyes close of their own accord, so I also get a couple of extra hours there too. My day is a full one, I get the maximum amount of time. I started doing this because—as with the quote by Bill Gates at the end of the last chapter—to fill my life as I want to do, to get my CV so heavy that it collapses tables, I need more time. I was first inspired to do this by Margaret Thatcher who I admired very much for her massive work ethic and her bottle. Politics apart, I have no interest, she's a gutsy lady. She used to manage incredible amounts of work and pressure and all on only four hours of sleep a night. That just awes me. Now, I don't imagine that she just suddenly said, 'That's it Dennis, I'm only sleeping four hours a night from now on you blighter.' I doubt that's how it worked at all. I suspect that she gradually cut her sleep a bit at a time until she was down to four hours. Similarly I never just started getting up at 6.30 a.m. I began by getting up at 8 a.m., then after getting used to that, 7.30 a.m., then 7 etc. I built myself up to less sleep until in the end, and as I stand now, I can manage very well on just six hours—and I'm still working at it, eventually I'll get it down to even less. Like the 'Four Yorkshire Men' (*Monty Python*), I'll probably end up rising for work in the morning before I go to bed at night. We're not here for long, I want to make the best of it, the very best. Margaret Thatcher had done half a day's work before most people even got out of their beds. I'm the same now. Most people are still wiping the sleep from their eyes and I've written another chapter, had a walk round the local park and spent an hour reading the morning papers at McDonald's, according to what my schedule is, with a hot coffee. Isn't that Nirvana? I can't believe when I'm walking around the local country park at 6.30/7 a.m. how lucky I am, I get the whole place to myself, I can't get my swede around the fact that the park isn't full of people taking the very same advantage. People are always complaining to me that they don't have enough time. We all have the same amount of time as Bill Gates, he only gets 24 hours you know, Richard Branson only gets 24 hours, Tony Blair the same. Winston Churchill? By all accounts he only got 24 hours too; it's how much of that time they used and how they used it that made them exceptional.

People also say to me, 'Yeah, but Geoff, I've got the kids and by the time I get home from my job, well, you know, it's not possible to do the things that I want and . . .' blah-de-blah. I know it can be hard, I've got four children myself who had to be brought up, I understand constraints but if you think like that, of course you will be constrained. In fact it was Henry Ford who said that, 'If you think you can or you think you can't you're right.' Because what we believe becomes our truth and if you say that it's impossible then you make it so. When I was on the door I was at one period in my life working a full day on the buildings, six nights on the door, training every day, writing articles, playing with my kids and also running a household. Sometimes I wouldn't get home from the nightclub until 3.30 a.m. and I had to be up again at 6.30 a.m. Often I was getting up for work before I went to bed at night (did I do that joke already?). And although that was pretty uncomfortable and I was stretching too far for good health, I did get loads done, I ran out of ink on my CV, my hard drive was full to overflowing.

I got more life experience in nine years than most get in a whole incarnation. When people read my bouncer books for instance, some don't believe how much I experienced, they feel I must be lying because there is so much. I have been accused more than once of making it all up. Which makes me smile because the books don't cover half of it. There were so many situations, so many that I couldn't, wouldn't or didn't want to include in the books, that I could have filled many more. My mates are always saying to me, 'Why didn't you put this situation in, why did you miss out that situation?' When you use your time properly, and I mean all the time you have, you get on the fast track, there is a quickening and you become the person you know you can become. Again, I don't recommend that you suddenly start working fifteen hours a day, it would be foolhardy to just jump in the deep end—you'll definitely make yourself ill. But start stretching yourself and start stealing more hours from your day. You don't have to sacrifice time with your loved ones if you do the majority of your work while they are still in bed. My kids are still asleep as I am writing these words, when they get up I'll give them all a cuddle and a kiss and have some jam on toast and a cup of tea with them before I take them to school and work. If I have to go places to teach I try and take them with me, or arrange the meetings so they land at a time when they're at school so they don't miss me too much. When my karate clubs were running many years ago and my kids were still little, I spent a lot of time at the clubs, but so did my children, they all went with dad to training and loved it. When Louis, my son, was only two or three he used to trail along to the karate class with me and wander around as I taught. The other practitioners would stop as he passed and hold the punching pads so that he could hit them. It was a wonderful time for the kids, there was no neglect of their time, they spent more time with me than most kids spend with their more conventional dads.

If your time doesn't suit you remember that it is your time, no one else's, you only hire it out to others. So what doesn't suit, change.

I'd like to tell you that if you manage your time really well that you can still *make* it working normal hours, but I'd be lying if I said that. I have never met anyone to date that didn't work their nuts off to become successful. That's the way it is. And it might sound daunting but really it isn't because when your work is your passion it doesn't feel like you are working at all. We recently had a very busy time with our mail-order business. We did a mail-drop to all of our lovely customers which entailed filling and stamping thousands of envelopes. It took us two days. Did I take that time away from my kids? No, my kids love the mail-drops because they all muck in. We all sit around filling envelopes, racing to see who can fill the most the quickest. Sharon will bring us all sandwiches and soup and drinks and we have a great laugh, it's an exciting time. And I always give the kids a wage, especially the younger ones, which makes them feel grown-up.

When you pursue your passion you fall into Salvador Dali's time and the hours fly. Salvador Dali did a beautiful painting of a melting clock that signifies his theory. One of my very good friends, Steve, brought me a coin with an engraving of the melting clock and I carry it everywhere with me as a reminder that 'time melts' when you are enjoying yourself.

Dali felt—he knew—that there were two types of time as we know it. Chronological time; seconds, minutes, hours that we measure, and the type of time of a melting clock. We have all experienced linear time. When we are doing something that we hate the clock ticks very slowly and days seem to stretch into weeks. If, however, we are with the girl of our dreams or we are pursuing a passion, the time just seems to melt away, it disappears and before we know it, hours have gone and they feel like minutes. So working twelve hours a day at the factory might drag like mad but when you are working twelve hours a day for yourself, time flies. It goes so fast in fact that you often tend to find yourself staying at the job even longer. People say that you're crazy and that you shouldn't work so many hours but it's not like you're working, it's great, you really enjoy it. I often look back at what I have achieved thus far and I realise that it couldn't have happened if I wasn't at the job for a lot more hours than I might be expected to do working for someone else, and there have been times when I have overworked, but I've loved every minute of it.

How many people can say that?

Rule Ten

Develop your talent!

Often the people that don't succeed blame the fact that they have no, or not enough talent, no gift. They look at those they aspire to be like and often feel cheated because these people are 'naturals', born with great ability, destined for success. I don't doubt that some people are born with natural talents and that some do take to new skills more easily than others.

I have met a lot of people with natural talent, but because it came so naturally they don't respect it and therefore fail to use it. We all know a brilliant footballer, or a gifted snooker player or an ace musician who never got beyond county level. Why? Because they didn't drive their talent, they didn't nurture and, Rule Ten: *'Develop their talent.'* They took 'no' for an answer when 'no' is not acceptable, and they failed to build on their skills. Many of the greatest talents in the world, in history, were not natural. Escher (he did the drawing of the eternal staircase and the hands drawing themselves) became one of the greatest artists of this century on a skill in drawing that, initially, his peers called 'interesting'. Interesting? If you took your very best work to one of your heroes for critique and he said 'interesting' wouldn't that make you feel like snapping your pencil and taking up lathe-turning?

Many years before Margaret Thatcher became Prime Minister conditions for women were so bad in politics that it was thought a woman Prime Minister was about as likely as a housing estate on the moon. Did that stop her from becoming the most recognised lady in the world? Read Branson's story, Gandhi's story, read Escher or Steinberg (another great artist), read about anyone of greatness and you'll find people that had really strong work ethics, but initially were all thought to be outsiders, even also-rans. Bill Gates is surrounded by computer geniuses that could talk him under the table as far as computer knowledge is concerned. They know a lot more than he does, and yet he is the richest man in the world because of his innovation in the computer world. Escher, even at his best, said that kids in high school could draw as well as he but they lacked the passion, energy and intuition that went into his work. He said, 'For the most part things like talent are mere poppycock. Any schoolboy with a bit of aptitude might draw better than I; but what is usually lacking is the unwavering desire for expression, obstinacy gnashing its teeth and saying, "Even though I cannot do it, I want to do it."'

When you buy an Escher, or even a print of

Escher, you don't get the best drawing in the world but you do get a piece of him because he placed his whole being into every drawing he ever did. I spent months trying to track down some of Steinberg's work. I read his obituary in *The Times* and was so intrigued by what the writer said about this great man that I wanted to see his work. When I eventually tracked down two books do you think I found the greatest line-drawer on the face of the earth, the greatest painter on the planet? No, I found drawings that kids in secondary school could better but I also found—and this is what I loved—Steinberg. He was alive in his work. He jumped out of the pages. He did one drawing of himself trapped behind his own signature, and I loved that. It just did something to me. He would draw sounds! I mean, what is that all about? How the heck do you draw sounds? He drew the sounds, using typography, of a car, of a truck, of a ringing phone, he drew country sounds too. And you look at these drawings of sounds and you can actually see them—you get it. He did one drawing of the sound of a raccoon and I could see it, it was amazing. But if you picked up Saul Steinberg's work and started looking for a technically brilliant drawing you'd be thinking, 'Somebody's having a laugh,' because he didn't do 'technical' but what he did do actually moves you. He was the same as many of the greats, he had, at first, a very basic talent and, irrespective of early criticism, he blasted a hole in contemporary art that you could drive a legion through. He was an amazing man.

Have you ever read or seen Jim Cartwright? I am lucky enough to count him as one of my best friends. Read Cartwright, or better still go and see his work at the theatre. Incredibly, some of his best work was written when still at school, and yet no one ever picked up on it because it was so unconventional. Often you would read it on the page and it wouldn't come off, but when it left the lips of a trained actor it set the stage on fire. It touches a part of you that has never been touched, it moves you. It isn't pretty, some of it smacks you in the eye and doesn't even say sorry but it absolutely knocks you off your chair when you read it. He places words together in such a way as I have never seen before and his stuff awes me.

I can also remember the story told to me by my lovely friend, John 'The Brush'. He's the guy who did the cartoons for this book. When he decided that signwriting was no longer for him, he got a portfolio together of all his best drawings and cartoons and approached the biggest agents in London to represent his work. After traipsing around from place to place being told the same thing in every office 'Your work's not good enough, leave your card in the bin.', he went home dejected. Now, if John had listened to the majority of people that day he'd still be kneeling in shit writing logos on the sides of ten-year-old delivery trucks. Instead, he picked himself up, took the advice that some of the kinder agents had given him (develop your art) and went on to become a gifted artist and one of the top cartoonists in the business.

Many of the real legends in life were not always the very best at what they did—certainly not in the early days. I think people tend to look at successful people and think, 'If I had that talent what could I do?' 'That talent' can be developed. Gandhi stumbled many times on his way to greatness, he was a crap lawyer by his own admission. He was 'sex mad' and felt controlled by his desires, to the point of visiting prostitutes (again by his own admission), and he was probably the least likely to succeed. Yet by going away and developing his talent, by turning a spark into a global flame he became one of the most powerful, most loved, respected and followed men in the known universe. He was wined and dined and admired by kings and queens all around the world. What Gandhi had, he made. It was not given, there was no gift, he didn't walk into power, he placed himself into the most unforgiving furnace and forged a man of mettle. Gandhi is probably the one man that I admire more than any—and he did it all without hurting a fly. When we say that someone is gifted, it is often with the implication that he or she didn't have to work for their talent and that they were just given it, 'it was a gift'. I believe that Gandhi's gifts were opportunity and time and we are all offered *them*, he just used his to the very best of his ability.

When I was at the factory, many years ago, I worked with a young lad called Olli. When he first came to work at the factory I was told what a brilliant footballer the lad was. To be honest, he didn't look much heavier than a football himself and I seriously wondered whether the stories of his soccer prowess were being exaggerated. That is until I watched the lad play. He could really kick a ball, and what a shot, very near broke your leg if you got in the way. It amazed me that he wasn't already a pro. I said to him one day, 'How come you don't do this baby for a living? How come you're not kicking a ball for your bread?'

'Well,' he said, 'I have had a couple of trials but I messed them up, out the night before on the beer, you know how it is. I've got another chance though, in a couple of months.' Apparently one of the bigger pro' sides had invited him down for a trial. 'That's really exciting,' I said, 'so how often are you training to get ready for it?'

He thought for a minute then said, 'Couple of times a week.' A couple of times a week! I wanted to grab the lad by the throat and point him at the lathes and mills and say, 'Is that what you want for the rest of you life; shit and grime and sweat and crap?' He had one opportunity really to do something, to sell his talent and place himself in an elevated position and he wasn't even training for it.

'If I was you right now,' I said, just managing to keep my cool, 'I'd be training at least twice a day to develop my skills and you wouldn't get me within a mile of a factory or a pub.' I just couldn't understand why he wasn't getting ready for the big day. I won't even tell you where this story ends because I reckon you already know. It's too depressing to even think about.

I have met a few like this who have had the chance, who had a raw talent and then thrown it away because they didn't develop it.

Billy Connolly, probably one of the greatest comic talents in the world today, started out as a shipyard worker in Scotland. A welder. He didn't start out as a genius comic; he wasn't remembered by his friends as being the funniest thing since Laurel and Hardy. He was just another one of the lads who liked to have a laugh. Initially he had dreams of being a folk singer, and for a while he did that quite successfully. One night on stage a string broke on his banjo, right in the middle of a song. As he tried to fix the string he had a bit of a joke with the audience; they laughed and a comic genius was born. From then on in Billy started to talk more and more to the audience between songs and tell them little stories, mostly ones he made up on the spot. These little stories became very popular so he started doing less singing and more chat. Eventually, realising that he had something, he went on to develop into what you see on your screens today. He also has a fabulous philosophy. I remember watching him on the Parkinson talk-show. He turned to the camera and the audience and said, 'You could do this, you could get up here and do this, anyone can do what they want.' When he said it, when he told the world, he was very emphatic, he really meant it. That's what I love about him, he was not being patronising, just being honest. He really believes that anyone who really wants to excel can. He knew it and wasn't afraid to say so. Michael Parkinson wasn't having any of it, 'Yes,' he said to Billy, 'but you have to have the talent, not just anyone could do it.' Billy Connolly looked at him and said something like, 'I was a welder who was a bit funny, I had to develop it, but anyone can do that.'

Talent can be developed. If you really want something and believe that you can have it, nothing will stop you, nothing will get in your way, no one will hold you back, even if ninety-nine out of a hundred say, 'Actually you're crap!' it still couldn't stop you if you were determined. The talent is almost secondary. Charlie Chaplin didn't just suddenly become the legend we see in the silent movies, he didn't just wake up one day with a contract to star in films that would be remembered forever, films that would lionise him. He started small, with a small talent that he developed by meeting others with greater talent, people that would nurture him and help him climb his Everest. He actually started as a stooge for the old wrestlers in the music hall. When one of the wrestlers, someone like Sandow or Hackenschmidt, would come on stage and ask for a challenge from the audience, Charlie Chaplin would stagger on— pretending to be a drunk—and proceed to comically bash the huge wrestler up, much to the delight of the audience. When you watch him on the silver screen, all you see is the matured and brilliant Chaplin, a master of mirth with awesome screen presence and comic timing. You don't see the young up-and-coming actor struggling for work, you don't see the little guy looking at his reflection in the mirror after yet another rejection letter asking himself, 'Will I ever get work?' Everyone started somewhere you know.

Look at some of the people singing on the TV. They're great, they're lovely people and I really admire them for getting to where they are. But many of them didn't get there on vocal ability. In fact some of them are pretty poor singers. Have you ever been at the local working men's club and watched a singer or a comedian or some other act and thought to yourself, 'They're better than the ones on TV,' have you ever done that? Well I'm going to let you into a little secret. You're right, they are better, sometimes much better. But they're still singing at the local working men's club and the others are on the TV. The ones that end up as the big stars are the ones that fine-tune their art by constantly taking a chance, by constantly stepping out of their depth to learn a new technique, a new line, a new angle. If you stick to playing at the working men's clubs then you'll always work, but only at the working men's clubs. When you get to the top at the working men's clubs it's time to start at the bottom somewhere else, or you'll never grow.

When Neil Adams, the brilliant judo master, reached the top in the Midlands he didn't stay there as king of the castle, he moved to London as a fifteen-year-old and started at the bottom again where he was thrown around and beaten up by the senior players.

It was harsh, but if he hadn't moved up he'd have stayed a good regional player and probably never have taken world honours. It wasn't long before he also reached the top of that class and had to travel abroad to get fights. At seventeen, he went to Japan where, again, he was one of the worst and not the best fighters in the class. A Japanese Judoka, who he nicknamed Gold-tooth, made a beeline

for this young up-and-coming player and proceeded to throw him—on and off the mat—from pillar to post. Again Neil felt out of his depth, but he stuck with it and it wasn't long before Gold-tooth got his just deserts. In the end he wouldn't even come on the mat when Neil was training. Neil didn't just become an Olympian, he wasn't born in a judo gi, he had to be a beginner the same as everyone else.

When Rigan Machado of the Gracie clan in America, a very famous grappling family, won the Brazilian ju-jitsu championship as a green belt, he was high on his success. He was the best green belt in Brazil. Did he stay there and rest on his laurels? No, he moved up into the senior class where he didn't win another fight for over a year. In the senior class he was able to take his skills to the next level, he was nurtured until he soon became the top of that class also. Then he had to move again and each time he got to the top of one class he moved to the bottom of another.

My mate, a budding writer, has been trying to get a script on the TV for years. He was watching a TV programme the other day and after about ten minutes he turned to his wife and said, 'This is terrible!'

She said, 'Yeah, but it's on the TV.' And she was right, it was on TV and he wasn't. So despite the poor quality, whoever had written it had made it happen, whilst my friend was struggling to get beyond the slush pile at the BBC.

It isn't your talent that counts most; it is what you do with the talent—no matter how little you think you might have—that really counts. And the funny thing is, once you do make it and you're up there, your talent seems to grow to meet the bigger arena.

It is attitude and not aptitude that determines altitude. You can be anything. Anything.

Rule Eleven

The secret of necessity and growth

The world is moving forward at a fast rate and often it feels as though we are playing catch-up. We get up in the morning and chase the minutes until nightfall when we go back to bed dreading the morrow. It's groundhog day, but it doesn't have to be this way, we can change it, we can get ahead and keep ahead, we can lead rather than follow, but only if we discover and use Rule Eleven: *'The secret of necessity and growth.'*

Have you ever heard that saying, 'If you always do what you've always done you'll always get what you've always got?' I mentioned it in my book, *Fear—The Friend Of Exceptional People* and it is really what this chapter is about. If you don't do anything other than what you are doing right now, how can you ever expect to get anything other than what you already have? To grow in life we have to 'grow with life'. We have constantly to be moving forward, onward and upward. If we are not moving forward we are moving backward because whether we like it or not, evolution is a forward-moving phenomenon—and in this decade that movement is at a rate of knots. In the last hundred years

174

civilization has moved ahead probably faster than in the last thousand years. There have been so many new inventions in this century that our technology has far outgrown our consciousness. We have moved forward so fast that even our survival mechanism, 'fight or flight', has become antiquated and, in my opinion, it is starting to damage and, in many cases, kill us as a species. So we have a lot of catching up to do just to keep a status quo.

Most people in life are reactive. That is, they react to outside stimuli and then play catch-up—or in many cases if they fail to catch up they die off. Many reactive businesses, that were once corporate giants, have actually become extinct because of their tendency to follow rather than lead. And in their turn, even the leaders that sit on their laurels and stop pioneering, perhaps because they think that they are far enough ahead to be safe, fail to evolve and go the way of the dinosaur. You can look at any industry to see examples of this. The pop industry is a classic. New talent hits the scene and excites us with its innovation. But then it finds a comfort zone, becomes caged by the fear of breaking its own standards and ends up in the archives gathering dust. It's incredible when you think of the amount of people that come and go in the pop world. Stars that once lit the sky now fail to even cause a glimmer. Many struggle even to get shows at the local working men's clubs and end up in the 'Where are they now?' section of a quiz show or on a compilation album of 'old greats'.

The opposite of this of course, are the giants that refuse to die because they encourage their creativity to grow and flourish, they write and sing for themselves and not for flavour-of-the-month sales forecasts. The Rolling Stones, Dire Straits, David Bowie, Michael Jackson, Tom Jones are just a few of the great artists that work ahead of their time. To be honest, this list is not as extensive as the list of those that have fallen by the wayside. Tom Jones is probably the very best example of moving with and ahead of the times. He manages to adapt his own unique style to the contemporary marketplace without selling out. He has re-invented himself time and again and is as great as he ever was.

Richard Branson is another great example of this constant climb, going from small record shops, using a public phone box as his means of communication, to record producing to . . . well what pie doesn't this marvellous innovator have a finger in? I love the guy. I highly recommend you read his book *Losing My Virginity*: it is one of the most inspiring books I have read.

So the key is to be proactive rather than reactive. To lead rather than to follow, to innovate rather than imitate. And it's one of those words that you hear so often that in many ways it has been overused, it's been done to death so when you hear it, it's easy to yawn and switch off. 'Proactive': the word hints at 'New wave, corny-city, OK yar' type philosophies that are about as useful as a tissue umbrella in a hurricane. But the truth is, it's the only way to be ahead of the game. Followers always get the hand-me-downs that the leaders toss away, the crust of the bread that no one else wants. They have to sit and watch as the leaders strip the carcass and just hope there might be a bit of meat left over. Leaders are also more secure—oh yes they are—even though they are constantly breaking comfort zones and facing the fear of doing so. They are more secure than the followers, because they are not sat there with their very popular product thinking, 'What if the bubble bursts? How would we manage if suddenly nobody wants to buy from us any more?' Successful people who rely on what they have are always insecure; they are living a precarious existence. There is a great Babylonian concept about obtaining wealth in its many forms that says we should always increase our ability to earn. I do this by constantly improving my skills and stretching into new areas, not necessarily too far detached from what I am already doing, perhaps the same in fact, just at a higher level, in the bigger circus. I can well remember sitting in a beautiful hotel in the gorgeous city of Edinburgh with my business partner, Peter. I was perturbed that, no matter how hard I seemed to work, I couldn't get higher in my business—at the time it was just martial arts books and videos. I had thought about it every which way and, although I had achieved much, I couldn't seem to take what I had any higher. Peter, who is two years older than water, a very erudite man, pointed out that I was already as high as I was going to get in that particular field and I had been hitting my head on the ceiling for a couple of years, without even realising it. He suggested that rather than keep hitting my head I should move my show to a bigger circus where the ceiling was higher, or where there was no ceiling at all. He told me a story about how ants are trained for the circus. If you want to train ants to perform in a circus, he told me, the very first thing you have to do is get them to stop jumping out of the arena. This is done by placing a glass ceiling above them so that every time the ants try to jump out they crack their little ant heads on the ceiling. Ingenious. After a few tries at jumping out of the circus the ants—clever little things—think, 'Hold on, every time I jump too high I hurt my swede. I know, I'll jump lower.' Once trained in the art of jumping low, the glass ceiling can be taken away without any worry of the ants trying to escape. They have banged their heads so many times that, even though the restriction has been lifted they no

178

longer jump out of the arena. And even the next generation of ants, following the example of their peers, don't jump higher than the imaginary ceiling.

I was like one of those little ants, hitting my head on a glass ceiling that I had installed myself. For some reason I felt that the martial arts were my circus, my whole world, and that I couldn't just up and go to a bigger one. I think that subconsciously I had failed even to see that there was another circus, and had begun to see the martial arts world as all there was. Once the realisation hit home, I packed my bags and moved to the bigger circus, I started expanding my skills to a more mainstream market. Now I still love the martial arts, I still train in them, but if I want my cerebral muscles to grow I have to take more weight on the bar.

In the martial arts market I was leading but fell into the trap of staying comfortable with my lead and stopped looking outside for a better way. Now that I am on the outside looking in, I can see very clearly that our only limitations are those that we place on ourselves or that we allow others to place upon us. If you think that you are a twenty-grand-a-year man, financially or metaphorically—or you allow others to make you feel that this is your worth—then that's your glass ceiling, you will always accept twenty grand a year and be grateful to be at the top of your tree. So when you go for a new job or a new contract and they say, 'What are you worth?' or 'What do you want?' you'll probably say something like, 'Twenty-one grand please.' Then keep your fingers crossed that they don't realise that actually you are only worth twenty grand. I read a story the other day about a chap at an interview for a great job. He was doing really well, impressing the board and making a good case for getting the job he was applying for until one of the interviewers said to him, 'So how much are you worth, what do you want us to pay you?' The guy hummed and ha'd and finally said, 'Well, I don't really know.'

'Well,' said the interviewer, 'what we'll do is give you the job and assess you. After a month we'll give you what you are worth.'

'You can't do that,' said the guy, all perturbed, 'I'm already getting more than that where I work now!'

If you say you're worth fifty grand a year, say it and mean it or don't say it at all. If you can't convince yourself, you are very unlikely to convince others. And make sure your confidence is well founded. It's no good thinking or saying that you're the best if you can't back that up. One German gentleman applying for a job as an English interpreter in Berlin was asked if his English was fluent, '*Ja*,' he replied, '*mein Englander ist ver goot*.' Needless to say the lad was not short-listed.

Know your worth

People, like animals, sense fear and insincerity. They also sense confidence, they know when you are worth more just by your presence and will probably be embarrassed to offer you any less than the top rate. You have to know your worth. A friend, an excellent plumber, had a call from a big potential client. He was in line for a very big contract that was worth a lot of money to his business, and it could have opened the doors to many more if he did the job right. The client asked, 'How good are you?'

My friend, being ever so slightly falsely humble, replied, 'Oh I'm not bad, I mean there are other firms bigger and better than me, I'm not the best, but I'm not bad.' He didn't get the job. Would you hire someone who was 'not bad'? I know I wouldn't. When you say what you are worth mean it. If you are not worth it go and get some more training until you are. Martin, a brilliant producer friend of mine, knows his worth. When asked to do a short production job he proffered his price (over the phone). When told that his price was too high he confidently told them that they must have been misinformed if they thought a producer of his standard would even get out of bed for any less. He then went on to offer them the phone number of a lower priced producer. They didn't use the number, they hired Martin. You must have a price that you won't go below. If people sense for a single second that you can be bartered with they'll chop you down until you are practically doing the job for nothing.

So, where was I? Talking about necessity and growth and ants and circuses. What I have always managed to do to keep me growing and stop mediocrity from getting its clammy claws on me, is to put myself under pressure by constantly expanding my goals, by constantly finding new Everests to climb and by injecting necessity so that the organism—me—grows.

Eight years ago I lived in a bedsit with nothing to my name but the clothes I stood up in and a half-eaten pork pie. This week I had my first payment for a film script I've written for cinema. I have achieved this by constantly expanding my fish bowl and then growing to accommodate it. It has been systematic and pyramidic growth. I didn't go straight from the fish bowl to the ocean. I didn't go from A to Z in one fell swoop, I didn't go from crawling around the furniture to running the New York marathon. It's a process, it takes time, I have had to be patient with myself and let the growth be organic. I climbed in manageable steps and I am still climbing. I did this by injecting necessity that encouraged growth. It's like lifting weights. If your goal is to be able to lift 300 lb above your head, you don't just walk into the gym, load the bar up and heave your guts out. That'd be dangerous, to say the very least, because the mind and the body are not prepared for that amount of weight. You won't lift 300 lb because your muscles are not strong enough to lift 300 lb; you haven't developed a 300 lb mentality. There has to be a preparation process. An attempt so early is likely to end in failure and subsequently discouragement.

Don't try to become Samson in a day, rather go to the gym and load the bar up with a weight you can easily manage and lift it above your head. This builds the musculature and your confidence. Very soon that weight is going to be too light, you'll lift it so easily it'll bore you. In life this is where most people stop! They learn to lift a weight above their head, metaphorically speaking, comfortably and have no inclination to go any further than that. The discomfort of trying to do a bigger lift puts them off and they end up as one of the very many millions that can lift x amount of weight above their head. However, for those of us that want to develop a bigger strength and a bigger lift, x amount is not enough so we add weight to the bar and start getting uncomfortable. Again, often people avoid discomfort but if you want to get big you have to shed your shell and open yourself up to the wide world.

Organic necessity

With organic necessity we react to stimuli that come into our lives and are forced either to grow or fall. If the boss at work thinks you can take more responsibility he might give you a promotion and extra workload. At first this is usually a struggle as you learn to cope with the new position, though after a while you settle in and a new comfort zone, a new shell, is formed, and everything is easily manageable once again. Similarly if you have a crisis in your life, your marriage breaks down, there is a death in the family or you lose your job, you tend to go from devastation through coping—though not necessarily well—right through to living comfortably with your new situation. You grow organically to cope with the necessity of life's demands. Waiting for situations to challenge you and then reacting is the way that most people get by—'get by' being the operative phrase. Because you are reactive as opposed to proactive you always tend to feel controlled by these situations, in some cases even blackmailed and overwhelmed by them; 'What if I lose my job, how will I cope? What if my wife/husband leaves me, how will I live?' etc. This equates to a stressful existence, always waiting for life to throw something at you and never quite sure if you will manage when it does. Often we live in fear of what 'might happen' even though 95 per cent of what we fear never does. In the end we become more controlled by the wild imaginings of anticipation than we do of anything actually happening.

This is one way to live, and the majority fall into this paradigm. The other way is to attack life, attack the things that we fear, sit with our problems until they offer us a solution instead of sitting outside them complaining that we have a problem. Problems are stepping-stones, they are great opportunities to grow, and they are ladders sent to help with the climb that we

185

all must take. I have realised this for a long time, though it is only in recent years that I have developed the wisdom and courage to not only meet my problems positively and use them to grow, but to also go out there and find problems/opportunities so that I can get on the fast track. Rather than wait for them to come and subsequently to live in fear of change, I have gone out there and sought them out.

I remember the story of a great though very vicious karate man in Japan who used to beat the shit out of any occidentals—foreigners, or gajin, as they were known by the Japanese— that went to the East to train in the Oriental arts. Most of the foreign fighters lived in fear of this very high-graded and brutal man. If he happened to visit the dojo (training hall) that they were practising in they would normally get beaten up, and then live in fear of it happening again. Many of this man's victims left Japan broken men, never again to regain their faith in human nature. One particular European man found this unacceptable, he refused to live in fear of this bully, so rather than wait for the inevitable visit he turned the tables on the Japanese fighter and went to visit him. The fight was a bloody one with the Japanese man coming a very sorry second place.

Similarly, when I was a young martial artist climbing the ladder to the top I always made a point of chasing my fears, of choosing the hardest partner and of always placing myself with a fighter who was faster, stronger and higher in grade than myself. Many of my friends thought this attitude suicidal—and I did take a couple of beatings it has to be said—but I figured that if at some point I was going to have to fight these guys anyway, I might as well do it on my own terms, when I wanted and not when they wanted. I also figured, and rightly so, that if I was only training with people of my own stamp or below I was very unlikely to get any better than I was already. If, however, I went with people much better than myself there was no limit to how good I could get. There was no ceiling on my potential. If you want to be a millionaire, as they say, then hang around with millionaires.

Injected necessity
Rather than wait for situations that would force me to grow (reactive), I actually go out and look for situations to force myself to grow (proactive).

When I want to improve at anything, anything at all, from writing right through to being a more Christian person, I seek out people that are ahead of my game to help in my quest. I go to classes where I am at the bottom of the pile and not the kingpin. Anyone can be great in his or her own little pool, but how many can swim in the big water?

When I wanted to be a good judo player I

didn't go to the local club to get to a good local level, I went and trained full-time with Neil Adams. For a year I was on the mat most days with eight to ten members of the Olympic judo squad. Every time I turned around I was fighting with a British Champion, a European Champion, even an Olympian. How could I not get good when everything around me was world class? How could I not shine when great lights surrounded me? I was also very lucky in the fact that all of Neil's lads are gentlemen and really looked after me.

Similarly, in business I am always looking to expand. To take my business from one level to the next, I moved premises to encourage the growth to happen. In my old premises I had eleven products that I sold via the bookshops and mail. In order to expand the business I moved to somewhere much bigger, somewhere that gave me a lot more space than I really needed. The new place was lovely but the mortgage was high and almost as soon as I moved in I remember thinking to myself, 'Blimey, I've got to write and sell a lot more books to justify this huge place, and to pay the mortgage.' I knew the bigger place, with more room and bigger bills, would force me to do exactly that. Within three years I went from eleven products to fifty-two products and the sales also went through the roof. I injected necessity by taking on a bigger place and the organism (the business) grew in accordance with it. Similarly, a little later, I started to order more books from the printers, five times more books than usual, and the reason was the same. If I order more books then I've got bigger bills to pay so I absolutely have to sell more books to meet those bills. I have to get out there and flog them like my life depends upon it otherwise I'm going to have bills from the printers that I can't meet. One week I had 20,000 books arrive on my doorstep from the printers. I said to Sharon, 'Crikey, there are loads of books. I've got to sell these quick.' So I immediately got my selling head on and started to flog the books. I got in touch with Peter the rep who kindly sells the books for me, and asked him how I could help him sell more books to the shops. He said it would help if the buyers (the bookshops) knew more about me so I started sending him copies of all the magazines that I wrote for or that had mentioned my work or me. Then I rang my distributor and asked, 'How can I sell more books?' They said it would help if I went out and met the bookshop owners and customers who bought my books, perhaps give public talks about my books. So I arranged to travel the country on a book-signing tour. I also revamped all my ads to make them better; I updated my web page (www.geoffthompson.com just in case you're interested). I rang up a lot of the suppliers that also sell my books and offered them bigger discounts if they bought in

189

bulk. Generally I worked my nuts and bolts off to meet the demands of necessity.

So inject necessity—not so much that you cannot cope, just enough to make you stretch—and then grow accordingly. When my mate Peter was telling me the ant story in Edinburgh (lovely city, did I say that?) he also told me how the trainers got the ants to jump if they were having a lazy day and thought, 'Naw, I'm not even gonna jump today.' The trainers would heat the bottom of their arena until they had to jump. Injecting necessity into your life and/or business is placing heat under your feet to make yourself jump. Just make sure that when you add pressure it is in accordance with what you can stretch to. Many people have taken a fall because they went too fast too soon. Remember that it is a process, and one of the most important factors in any process is time. Often it is the most pivotal thing, and when things take time you need patience.

I read the biography of Muhammad Ali where he talked about this process. Some of the fighters he met in the square ring scared the living daylights out of him—although of course he didn't let them know that—and often he felt so scared that he didn't want even to get in the ring with them. So he placed pressure on himself by publicly announcing that he was the greatest and that he was going to beat so-and-so in such-and-such a round. He would say this even though at times he didn't believe he could do it. By making these bold claims (injecting necessity) he was forced to deliver or look a right idiot if he didn't. This had a massive effect upon him. He trained like crazy, got the very best sparring partners, trained more than his opponents and harder than his opponents, and he also trained at times (very early in the morning, on holidays etc.) that his opponents would refuse to train. When he first made his claims he wasn't the greatest, but having made the bold claims that had the whole of the sporting fraternity glued to their TV screens come fight night, he had to come through with the goods, and eventually he did become the absolute greatest there ever was.

I remember a great story about Arnold Schwartzenegger when he first started out. He was almost unknown to the general public. He had written a book about fitness that he wanted to get into the bestsellers. Now, at the time, fitness books were not notoriously great sellers, they're still not, certainly they were not bestsellers. A company printing a book such as this might expect to sell 5,000 if they were lucky. Arnie knew that unless he came up with something superhuman his books would sell only a few thousand and then disappear into obscurity like so many others before him. He also knew that no one could sell the book quite like he could. No matter how good the selling rep was he could never do the book the justice Arnie felt it deserved. He put his thinking cap on and came up with the idea of literally selling the book himself. He arranged a massive book-signing tour of just about every city in America and then proceeded to visit each one. He gave talks, demos, he chatted with the customers, and made the staff laugh. He did everything next to actually taking the money from people's pockets and ringing the till. He knew that touring the whole country would be a huge stretch; he also knew that it would push him probably harder than he had been pushed before but he set the dates irrespective of this; once he was committed to them, he just went out there and did it. He took America by storm and by the end of the tour his book made it to number one in the New York bestseller list. He made it a bestseller by injecting necessity so that the organism responded. It was a massive effort, but then Arnie is a massive man.

When I first started making martial arts videos with Peter he taught me an invaluable lesson. For those that might not know, making videos is very hard, laborious work. I haven't met anyone yet that really likes doing it. There is loads of preparation, then you've got to stand in front of the camera and do your stuff, which can be very daunting until you get used to it, then you have the post-film editing which is absolutely soul destroying. When we first started making videos, before the very first one, Peter said to me, 'I can't understand why more people in the martial arts are not making instructional videos.' After our first one he said, 'Now I know why!' It was dead hard. Anyway, I digress. Once we had decided to make our first instructional video together we hummed and ha'd over when we should do it. We'd talk about a date and then put it off for another, and before we knew it several months had passed by and we still hadn't filmed a single frame. Peter rang me up one day and said 'Geoff, have you got your diary close by?'

'Yes.'

'OK, how are you fixed on x date?'

'That's a good date for me.'

'Right, that's the day we do the first video!'

BANG. That was it, we set the date. I was crapping myself but I was committed and had to do it. The video man had been booked, we'd hired a room to film, everything was in place and we just had to do it. And we did. Thirty videos later and that's the process that we still use.

Sometimes Peter will even pay for an advert for several months ahead (usually in a magazine) to promote a book that he hasn't even written. This always acts as a kick up the backside because if the ad came out and he didn't have a book, he'd lose money on the ad and also he'd have to send back the money that people sent for the book. This very thought makes him rush to the keyboard to get the book ready for the self-imposed deadline.

Rule Twelve

Integrity (the master rule)

This is just a personal one, because I know that for every one honest businessman and purveyor of life there are also dozens of dishonest ones. But I feel that if anything is worth achieving it is worth achieving honestly and with integrity. One of the men I most admire in life, David, he is retired now, gave me the piece of advice that he felt he owes his vast wealth to. He said, 'Use integrity in all things.' In fact, he says he owes his wealth to this one oft-abused concept, therefore Rule Twelve is: *'Integrity is the master rule.'*

I always ask David for advice when he is in the country and of all the sound bites he offers, this he says, is the most important. Never trick anyone, never knowingly fiddle anything, never employ dishonesty, not even on a subtle level, and always pay your taxes. If you find that you are doing business with someone and they have left a clause in the contract that you could take advantage of, point it out to them, show them their error. Your honesty in all matters is imperative to peace of mind and long-term security. I haven't met a single person yet who fiddles others and who is actually happy with their lot.

They are always looking over their shoulder for comebacks—especially with the taxman—and they never seem fully to enjoy what they have. Look at all these sportsmen and women at the moment taking steroids and performance-enhancing drugs. They are not gold medal winners, they are not champions and no matter how much they rationalise and say, 'They all do it so it's all right,' they are still cheating. They have still stolen their medals; they will never sit and completely enjoy their achievements because they are ill-gotten. I'm not judging, this is an objective truth. If the rules of the game say that performance-enhancing drugs are banned then you choose to cheat when you take them.

So honesty in all things is an imperative. Life is a reciprocal experience; we are constantly receiving that which we have given out. Think of your actions as a boomerang; what you throw out is what you get back. If you want to retire to the Bahamas like David and enjoy the fruits of your labour then make sure your labour is honest. This is such a subjective concept because of course there are many truths, each according to the person's knowledge. So the rule of thumb is intention. If you know something is wrong but still decide to do it, your conscience will bear heavy sooner or later, when reflection kicks your arse every time you try to enjoy what you have. If you act with good intention, not knowing that what you are doing is wrong at least you can look back and say, 'Well, I can see now that I was wrong, but at the time I didn't know any better.'

We often think it's clever when we manage to fiddle people or businesses out of a little bit of this or a little bit of that but really it's all dead petty. What we get away with really does nothing to enhance our quality of life at all, it just adds to the karmic debt that, at some time or another, has to be repaid. Even if you are given too much change at the supermarket, offer it back. If I order twenty slabs from the builder's yard for my garden and they send me thirty by mistake I'll ring them up and inform them of their error. I don't want an extra ten

196

slabs, no matter how free they are. I recently had the wing mirror on my Land Rover smashed off by a passing motorist, my friend offered to get me a new one, 'for next to nothing'. He knew a guy that could fiddle them out of the factory. At the risk of upsetting him I declined the offer and bought a new one. If it isn't honest I don't want it. Again I may sound judgmental, I may sound as though I am taking a higher moral ground. which I guess I am, but I am talking from experience. At one time, before I went into business for myself, I'd buy anything warm or even red-hot, I didn't care where it came from as long as it was cheap and I could make a killing on it in the re-sale. I'd rationalise it however I could to make my conscience lighter and I'd tell myself that it was OK and that 'everyone did it' and that it wasn't actually stealing—but it was. If you take it cheap, knowing that it's hot, you may as well have gone into the house or the shop and nicked it yourself. When I refuse to have anything bent I do it for the right reasons, not to be holier than thou; I do it because I am responsible for my actions, and the consequence of those actions. Life is like having a credit card with no spending limit, you can put as much on it as you like but at the end of the month you are the one that has to foot the bill because it all comes back to you invoiced and stamped with a due date to pay. That's if you are flippant or foolish with your actions. If, on the other hand, you are responsible with your actions the bill comes in at the end of the month with full credit and no karmic debt. What you give out is what you get back. In terms of bad, you get back everything that you give—sometimes more. With good, however, what you give comes back tenfold. Have a look at this next bit; it's an extract from my book *The Formula* and it is all about this aspect of integrity, giving to others with no profit.

'I expect to pass through life but once. If, therefore, there may be any kindness I can show, or any good thing I can do to any fellow being, let me do it now, and not defer or neglect it, as I shall not pass this way again.'

William Penn

Did you ever hear the DJ introducing the pop star with the perfunctory, 'does a lot for charity, but doesn't like to talk about it'? Well guess what, he just talked about it.

Giving to others should be, as much as possible, an anonymous event. Not giving so others can see how giving you are, or giving to ease conscience or as a publicity stunt, so that others might like you more, or to ease guilt or to hide shame. To give is a beautiful expression of love, but to give for tangible profit is just to exchange one form of currency for another.

Helping someone with a good deed is our greatest expression of love, until you sit and tell others what a great person you are because you did the good deed. Please don't misunderstand me here; I am as guilty as the rest. I've done some lovely things for others and then ruined it by telling someone what a great bloke I am for doing it. Giving completely free is hard, but something we should learn to do. It should be done because it is right, not because it makes a great CV or TV or because our mates will like us more or whatever.

When we give for free there is profit enough in the fact that our internal parent rewards us with feelings of wellbeing and self-worth.

There is also a contradiction in play here; I'm aware that, sometimes, giving to charity and helping others has to be publicised to encourage others to do likewise. I believe this is a good thing, as long as those involved remember why they are doing it: that it is the people and not the ratings that count. Who cares about the ratings; did you actually help someone when you used your name to promote a charity? That's what matters.

Giving to others is where most of our energy is generated, when we give it comes back tenfold and allows us to give more and to channel the self-perpetuating energy into our life goal.

'The most sublime act is to set another before you.'

William Blake

This is the best energy of all, the greatest energy we can reap. Everything we do in our life should ideally be aimed at this one single thing—helping others.

Your life goal might be directly working with others and helping on the ground floor. Or it might be to write a screenplay that touches and subsequently helps millions. As a professional football player your aim might be to achieve greatness on the world stage, but when you net the goal that wins the World Cup, how many people is that going to touch, to indirectly help, to inspire on their own path to greatness? Let me tell you that it would be a lot of people. Think of giving as an investment that cannot fail, a bet you cannot lose, an infinite pool of energy that can be dipped into any and every time. The more you give the more you get back.

So if it is such a sure bet why do we not give more, why don't we share our energy more often? Probably because most people have forgotten, or possibly not learned, that giving is all that there is, it is the single most important thing we can do as a species. We are here to serve, but the beauty is that when we serve others we also serve ourselves, what we

200

give out is what we get back. The best way then actually to get what you want from life is to help others to get what they want. So why not help more and why give out rubbish when that is exactly what we will get back?

Today is the first day of the rest of your life, a great time to re-invent yourself and become a giver. Once you get into it, it's very infectious, you'll want to do it more and more. It's like money in the bank that keeps growing the morc you give away. You give away a pound, a dollar or a yen and it comes back as ten pounds, ten dollars or ten yen.

One pound's worth of energy is not going to get you too far along the road to your goal, but ten pounds surely is. So give and keep giving, but try and give where it is needed, wanted and appreciated otherwise you could waste valuable energy. The Bible says do not cast your pearls before swine. It's not hard to know who is ready for it and who is not, no one needs to tell us because we will innately know. Usually when someone needs something from you they'll cross your path and you'll know. You don't have to go knocking on the doors of strangers, or helping old people cross a road they don't really want to cross. People that want help are all around us; start with them. Localise your philanthropy. My friend, infused by a giving spirit, told me how he wanted to save a rainforest to help others. I said, 'Why don't you start by simply helping others directly. Your secretary who can't cope with her workload, your daughter who needs parental guidance, or answer the letter that's been sat there for a lazy month on your desk. There are a million people that you can help, and they're all around you—build up to the rainforest.' I told my wife that I wanted to help others but that I didn't know where to start. She pointed out that I had ten letters from people that had written to me actually asking for my help and advice—why didn't I start there? I was so busy looking for someone to help that I didn't actually see those that had crossed my path. It was like I was saying, 'I haven't got time to help you, I'm too busy trying to find people to help!'

Work from the inside out; help yourself first, if you're not right, how can you help others? It'd be like the blind leading the blind. Help those closest to you, your family and friends, then extend to those outside the family unit and, depending upon how much you want to achieve, eventually to as many people in the world that you can. A sportsman, celebrity or big businessman, for instance, has the opportunity to help people on a world scale; what a fantastic opportunity. I often wonder if people, especially famous people, actually realise the power that one word, or one letter, or one phone call, or one acknowledgement could mean to someone that holds them in high esteem. These people are potentially so powerful that they could, between them, actually change the course of millions of lives. They have collected so much energy on their journey that they can give life and infinite energy with very little effort.

The legendary wrestler George Hackenschmidt was one such man. He always had time for those less fortunate. He touched and changed many lives for the better, often with as little as a comment or a compliment or a piece of advice. It was Mother Teresa who said, 'Let us not be satisfied with just giving money. Money is not enough, money can be got, but they need your hearts to love them. So, spread your love everywhere you go. First of all in your own home; give love to your children, to your wife or husband, to the next door neighbour.'

Giving needs to be practised so that it becomes a habit. A book such as this might give you the energy to get the ball rolling, but then you have to keep the momentum. Once you do this, the ball will find perpetual motion and roll itself. I'll finish the chapter with the profound words of Lau Tzu who advised us that, 'Kindness in words creates confidence. Kindness in thinking creates profoundness. Kindness in giving creates love.'

Rule Thirteen

The hidden power of books

I have discovered to my pleasure Rule Thirteen: *'The hidden power of books.'*

What we need to help us rise above the crowd is information. Actually I stand corrected because I know plenty of people with information by the bucketload but for whatever reason they do not employ it. I also know people that use their information but they use it wrongly. Wisdom is the correct use of information. One of the best ways to collect information and of course inspiration and aspiration, is books. When I spend hundreds and hundreds of pounds on books I consider it an investment in me, the person most likely to get me where I want to be. In books we have the opportunity to access the knowledge of a thousand lifetimes and assimilate it until it becomes us. I am a living embodiment of what I have experienced and a big part of what I have experienced is through the medium of reading. I always tell my little lad when he is struggling to get into a book that readers are leaders, small libraries make great men. And it is something that I believe emphatically. I have yet to meet a hugely successful person that wasn't a voracious reader. I even took a speed-reading course so that I could get through more material. It's all out there just waiting for you, and if you go to a public library it's absolutely free.

Can you imagine that, all that knowledge, all the secrets, all that information for the price of a few beers and a curry? I've spent up to £50 on a single book if it is the one that I am looking for. People often say that the only way out of the rat race is through football or sport or pure luck, it's not true, the best way out is through the library. Just imagine any great name or think of the person that you most admire, the person that you most aspire to be like, the one that makes you feel inspired just at the mention of their name. Mention any name and I'll almost guarantee that you'll be able to find their whole life, lock, stock and (two smoking) barrels; highs, lows, successes, failures, likes and dislikes, the secrets to their success and all between the pages of a book. They give you their whole life for maybe £15. The sum of their life, every lesson that they ever learned, every gem that they found all for a few quid. Now if that is not offering it all on a plate I don't know what is. I find it absolutely incredible that you can go into any bookshop (or even on the web—www.amazon.com) and buy the lives of the greatest men and women in history. You can find out why and how single individuals changed the course of history.

*It's all there, waiting to point you in the
right direction*

William Wallace—one man—saw a whole
village slaughtered and decided that he was
going to do something about it. He told his
wife; she said, 'But you're only one man.' That
one man changed the course of history with his
tenacity and courage. Mother Teresa—have
you read about this great and saintly woman?
About how she cared for thousands and

touched the hearts of millions? Just an ordinary girl who did extraordinary things, a village girl who touched the heart of the whole planet. What about the courage of Churchill, the tenacity of Thatcher, the wisdom of the Dalai Lama, the power and love of Sai Baba, the focus and dreams of Bill Gates, the rise and fall of Bonaparte? The list is absolutely endless. And it is all there waiting to point you in the right direction, all these extraordinary men and women saying, 'Let me tell you what I've learned from my life.' What an incredible opportunity. I am sitting here at this moment with a book of drawings by Saul Steinberg staring up at me. Steinberg isn't dead; he is alive and kicking in my office. He sat here, alive in his work, saying, 'What can I do for you Geoff, what can I teach you about my life through my work? Ask me, I'm here.' Did you know that Escher lives with me? You're damn right he does, and he only cost me about twenty quid. It was an absolute steal I have to tell you. A steal. He is here with me now. All his drawings and all his words. When I am feeling a little insecure about my work he is there to help me. 'Listen Geoff,' he tells me, 'we all feel insecure at times. I went on to become a world-renowned artist but there wasn't a day when I didn't doubt my work, there wasn't a day when I didn't think, "Is this any good?"'

Escher has taught me that insecurity driven

into your work is what makes it great, the very fact that the great Escher can doubt his work, can feel insecure, can feel like giving it all up, makes me feel that I am not on my own and that it is OK to have bad days and that an ordinary person can reach the stars. I remember first looking at his work and being filled with awe. I'd never have believed that he would have had any insecurities at all about this great art, but in his book he said, 'I've absolutely no reason to moan about the "success" of my work, nor about the lack of ideas for there are plenty of them. And yet I'm plagued by an immense feeling of inferiority, a desperate sense of general failure; where do these crazy feelings come from?'

I have Gandhi's life story in front of me. The book costs about eight pounds, the price is so little that I am almost embarrassed to say it. I spend more than that on crisps and sweets for my kids in a single week. Yet this one book has given me more direction and more hope than any amount of money. Gandhi has taken me behind the scenes of his life and shown me the rights and the wrongs, he has given me the secret to inner power, he has taught me that faith in yourself and your God means immortality, it also means that nothing is beyond you once you decide to ride the bull. He has shown me that I only have to master one single thing in my life and I can have anything I want. That one single thing is: me.

Gandhi learned how to lead himself, and he made loads of mistakes along the way, and by doing so he built up a personal following of over twenty million people. Can you imagine that? And reading his book taught me that I could, you could, and we all could do exactly the same thing.

*   *   *

Phew. I need a rest. I'm off for a cup of tea.

*   *   *

Right I'm back, where was I? Books. There are only so many things we can learn from one lifetime, only so many lessons we can learn with the finite years that we are allotted. Not enough time really. That's why books were invented, so that you can take a thousand great men and learn the lessons they learned from their lives. If you discipline yourself and get a lot of reading done you can become the manifestation of a thousand great men. You can learn all the reference points they offer and learn from their mistakes, you can take what it was that made them legendary and make it a part of you. These people have left their stories, their 'instructions for life' so that you can get on the fast track, so that you don't have to do the thousands of experiments they had to do to learn what they learned. Once you have acquired this knowledge you can use it to power your own journey of discovery. If you wanted to get around London the best thing to do would be to buy a street map. The biographies of great people are simply that, street maps to life. They have departed to another plane and left you the schematics. It's great. It's so wonderful. All you have to do is get out there and buy the books, read the stories and learn the lessons, then put them into action of course, don't forget to do that otherwise you'll end up with a mind full of useless information.

If you make reading a habit it'll be the best habit you ever made.

Rule Fourteen

Handling criticism

The other crabs

With success always follows criticism, from those below, those above and even those on the same level. And if you don't understand it, if you allow it to get inside your head, it can, at the very least, spoil your success; at worst it can kill your success. Rule Fourteen therefore, *'Handling criticism'*, is imperative.

It took me ages to pluck up the courage to even try to become a writer. When I left the factory after all those years (my mates at work nearly had a fit, they all said things like, 'he'll be back' and 'it won't work' etc.) it did raise my self-esteem and it did expand my belief system, but not enough at that time for me to believe I could be a writer. I went through many different jobs, from shovelling on a building site, to hod-carrying, brick-laying, demolition, sales and, eventually, nightclub doorman. I loved it all and even though none of the jobs fulfilled me, they did eventually give me the confidence to chance my arm as a writer. I went the scenic route it has to be said; hopefully through this book I might have been able to convince you that there is a quicker way, a motorway route.

211

It wasn't all plain sailing, I had my share of setbacks, not least of which was the reaction of the other crabs. One of my greatest disappointments with succeeding and aiming for the stars was to find how badly the other crabs behaved when I left the basket. I have watched so many people make their bid for success only to settle for the lathe because they allowed others to criticise and tell them it was all they deserved; even to the point where—in the absence of their 'friends'—they, like I, started to tell themselves the same thing. Failure became their norm and many gave up the race even before the starter's whistle.

When I first published *Watch My Back* a very close friend became overly abrupt and critical, even down-right rude. He told me that no one liked my work, he suggested that I shouldn't get above my station and, 'Whatever you do, keep your feet on the ground.' Another mate (I had great mates me!) told me emphatically that getting my first book published was a fluke and that I shouldn't let it go to my head. People I hardly knew told my friends, 'Oh yeah, Geoff Thompson, you can't speak to him now that he's made it. Who the hell does he think he is?' People asked me, 'Why can't you be happy in the factory like everyone else, you think you're someone, don't you?' Then went on to inform me that, 'People like us don't write books.'

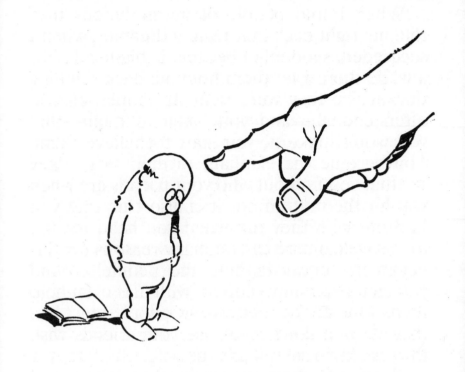

People like us don't write books

They pounded at my self-esteem like a lump hammer and, I must admit, even to this day and especially when I am tired, those old negatives still try to attack me.

Not only did people try to hold me back, some were, and still are, absolutely and unequivocally insulted that I thought myself worthy to the task. And every time my self-esteem grew, just a little, they clubbed it back like a beached seal. At times I cried with the frustration of it all.

When I told people of my ambitions they told me right back that I was a dreamer, when I succeeded, suddenly I became a 'big head'. For a while there I let them hold me back thinking that maybe they were right. If people tell you often enough—and you listen to them—that you won't make it, you start to believe them. You become the elephant to their twig. They say that you find out who your friends are when you hit the bottom but it is also true that you find out who they are when you head for the top as well. There can be many reasons for this negativity, understanding the people around you can help you to cope it with and even help them. One of the reasons why people react like they do is jealousy; because your friends wish they could do as well as you.

Then of course there's the green-eyed monster in all of us, envy. Friends often go green because you have reached a place where they would love to be. The obvious reason (and one that we tend to overlook) is fear. Close friends and relatives often fear that your success will leave them out in the cold, that you will no longer want them if you 'make it', and they show their fear by trying to hold you back in any way they can. Normally by trying to hold you back they inevitably lose you anyway, because when you place a cage around someone all it does is make them want to escape. The cage in effect takes away your free will. Then when you do escape they tell everyone, 'See, I told you he wouldn't want to know me once he made it.'

There is also the dreaded insecurity that we probably all feel from time to time. The reason why lots of people do not or will not grow, is because they feel secure in their comfort zones. A part of that security comes from the fact that most of their friends and relatives share the same zone. So when you expand and leave they often feel perhaps unconsciously like you have deserted them. Their security is threatened.

Resentment is a common factor. My growth out of the comfort zone caused a lot of resentment, especially from friends and some of my training companions who thought, in some cases knew, that they were as good as me, if not better, even though they hadn't chosen to do anything with their talent. They put my success down to pure luck, 'You're lucky that you got a break,' one told me.

'Yeah, you're right,' I replied, 'I was lucky. And do you know the funny thing, the more I work the luckier I seem to get.' People will give you a million sob stories about how they could have made it if only they got a break. In this world you have to make your own breaks, even the Bible tells us that God helps those who help themselves. Get out there and ride the bull or be content to watch from the bleachers. You can be a spectator or you can be a player—it's your choice. If you choose the former try not to criticise the player because he is in the arena and you are not.

Often I find that when a person outgrows those around him/her it can cause disorientation to those left behind. This is another reason why people stay in safe zones; it's because they fear change. Change causes disorientation. They feel fear at the edge of the comfort zone and associate everything 'outside' as fearful. In reality the fear and the discomfort are transient, once you have exited the comfort zone, escaped the womb as it were, the fear and disorientation dissipates. The sad thing is that if you change and you are an integral part of other people's comfort zone this will also cause them disorientation. Metaphorically speaking it's like you are standing up in the rowboat because you want to move to a better position, but as this rocks the boat for everyone else on board they say, 'Sit down and don't rock the boat.' It can also cause aggression if your loved ones, your friends, others in your community, or even complete strangers watching from the periphery become angry. Why? Because you've succeeded and they think you're pretentious for doing so or for even trying. You have moved on, grown, and unfortunately they haven't. You are a constant reminder of this fact. When they look at you and your success all they see is a reflection of their perceived failure.

I know that when I first hit the martial arts scene I inadvertently upset a number of people. Some took an instant dislike to me even though we had never met. Many would get very angry and irate, yet they knew nothing about me at all other than the snippets in the magazines. I remember one particular guy that actually despised me, he hated me to pieces. People said to him, 'Geoff Thompson's a nice bloke, what's up with you?' But he wouldn't have any of it. I didn't know anything about this at the time, the story was told to me later. Then one Sunday morning I happened to be teaching a course in this chap's neighbourhood and he decided to come along—'just as a spectator'. He told his friends, 'There's nothing this guy can teach me.' At the end of the seminar his whole attitude had changed and he approached me for a chat. Apparently I made a bit of a fuss of him and next time he saw his mates he was raving to them, 'That Geoff Thompson is a top bloke.'

If I had never got to meet this man he probably would always have despised me, and all because I was swimming against the stream and he wasn't. Anyone that goes against the crowd is likely to get the crowd going against them.

So the remedy, if possible, is to explain to your friends and loved ones that you love and need them as much as ever but their reticence

217

to let you 'fly the nest' is hampering your growth and causing you to resent them.

I was almost at the stage of giving up on one of my friends because of his anger and resentment towards me when I first started writing. One day I cornered him and asked him why he was being so negative about me. Every time I saw this particular friend he'd make me feel guilty and depressed by putting down my efforts to try and better myself.

As a last-ditch attempt at keeping the friendship alive I rang him up and we arranged to meet and talk things out. When I confronted him about his behaviour he said, 'Well, I'm your mate. I'm just trying to keep your feet on the floor, stop you from getting big-headed. Someone has to.'

I said, 'Look, I'm thirty-three years old, I'm a grown man, I don't need anyone to keep my feet on the floor and if my mates can't be a little more supportive with me then what kind of mates are they? I'm getting to the stage where I don't want to be in your company any more because you make me feel so depressed.' This came as a shock to him, he obviously didn't realise that his constant barrage of put-downs was having such a bad effect on me. Realising this he got his act together and became less critical and more supportive.

The moral of this little story is: try to understand those who are not growing with you and reassure them. If you can't make them see, and very often you cannot, then it is inevitable that you will have to move on. If you do, don't take any resentments with you. It's not personal, it's just a part of growing. Remember the good aspects of the relationship and move on. They will probably tell everyone that it's your fault and that you changed and that success went to your head and blah-de-blah; you've heard it all before, don't get upset about it, try to understand people and move on. You see it in the papers every day with famous celebrities whose friends and ex-loves crawl out of the woodwork to tell the world how they were deserted as soon as the famous person made it.

One thing that you are sure to attract as soon as you start doing anything out of the norm is criticism. Unfortunately it is unavoidable. But before we start to get too depressed about it there is a positive side. The fact that people are criticising usually means that you are on the right path. After all, no one kicks a dead dog. As soon as you put your head above the crowd you are shooting practice for the insecure. People who see you as some kind of threat usually fire the bullets of criticism. And the angrier their critique the more insecure and fearful you can be sure they are. Normally when others pipe up and slag you off they tell people more about themselves that they do about you. What I find

works well for me against the critic is absolute
indifference. Many critics get off on the fact
that they are criticising you and love others to
know that they have the bottle (in their own
mind) to do it. If you answer back and get into
a war of words and often worse, you are not
only wasting energy like throwing money down
the drain, you are also giving them their claim
to fame, you are actually placing them on your
level, or dropping to theirs. If they are
spending their life criticising you or other
people they do not deserve such a lofty
pedestal. And if you find yourself hurt and
firing back with all guns a-blazing then maybe
you are on the wrong level also. Success means
being ready to take the crap. If you are not
ready for that, then you are not ready to grow
yet. When you understand people, which I do,
you understand that aggression and anger and
'mud-flinging' are not the signs of maturity or
wisdom, not the signs of bravery or strength
but the signs of weakness and fear and
insecurity. When you understand this, you do
not feel the need to reply, or to be hurt, or to
feel threatened or damaged. You feel the urge
to do nothing other than ignore what is being
said and move on. I love the old Arab adage
and I live my life by it because I will never be
stopped on my journey by the insecurity of
others, 'The dog barks but the caravan moves
on.'

The dog can bark as much as it likes but this caravan is not going to stop for anything or anyone, I am just going to keep on moving and hit my destination. So I make a point of never answering my critics unless they have something of value that might help me. Now and again some good advice can come from the mud-throwers, sometimes there is a gem in the rocks they throw. If there is, take it out, shine it up and move on. One guy rang me up once to criticise something he disliked about me. After listening to him for a minute I said, 'You know what, you're right, and I appreciate your ringing to tell me.' He was right and I learned loads from the phone call, I also admired the fact that he spoke to me personally instead of behind my back, or through the magazines. If I didn't agree with him I would still have respected his opinion, even though I wouldn't have taken a lot of notice.

Don't throw rocks back because if you do, you drop back down to their level. The best thing you can do to critics when they throw mud is allow them their voice and then completely ignore them. Act as though they never existed; act as though the critic is an ant telling an elephant he's not strong. Do you think an elephant would feel threatened by an ant? I doubt it. The eagle does not take advice from the crow. If you let criticism hurt you it'll steal energy like a robber in the night and hold you back on your journey. If you start having a cat fight they know they have got you and they will keep attacking. Don't waste your time. Of course it is very easy to say, 'Don't react and don't be hurt!' Like you can just switch these emotions on and off tap-like. You can't. I know that, it took me ages to stop the bullets from finding their mark, and in the early days I took the bait hook, line and sinker. Now I have learned to build a shield around me that stops the shit from even touching the sides. Now the criticism may come, it may try to penetrate, but I don't allow the bullets to get anywhere near me. This is something that I have learned and practised over a long period. I still work on it every day. It is a part of my internal 'tree-training'.

Strong like the oak
One day, many moons ago, I was walking through the country park thinking about why criticism hurt me so much and how I could develop a strength that might help defend me from the crap-throwers (they were pretty crap too come to think of it). As I was thinking I looked at this beautiful and huge oak tree. I leant against the tree and remember thinking, 'Wow!' it was so powerful. So I asked the tree how it got so strong and impervious to the weather and to life (I did actually ask the tree, I kid you not). As I contemplated, a voice in my head said that the tree was so powerful because its roots were very deep and the layers of its skin were many. As the layers got deeper they got harder until, right at the centre of the tree, the core, the wood was like iron. Paradoxically, on the outside, the bark of the tree was relatively soft; you could even punch it without hurting your hand. So what was soft to touch was immovable, what was gentle on

the outside was like rock on the inner level, and the deeper you went the harder it got. But the tree that so impressed me didn't just suddenly become this huge oak, it started as an acorn, as a seedling, and grew over a long period of time becoming immovable, for the growth of the oak was a process. The weather that had attacked it had tempered it, what had seemed harsh to the younger tree was, in retrospect, actually kind. I wrote this poem about the oak:

The bark of the tree was condemning the
weather,
The branches and leaves at the end of their
tether.
The wind and the rain and the scorch of the
sun
Were the bringers of pain and the killer of
fun.
The weather replied (clement and not),
'We must disagree for we fear you've forgot,
That the rain sent has fed you from root up
to leaf,
And the sun sent has offered a summery
relief,
The storms sent have tempered a hell of a
bloke,
And built you right up from the acorn to
oak.

I felt that I could learn from this, I felt that,

like the tree, the things that tested and hurt me would also temper me, and more quickly if I realised that the process was a necessary part of going from acorn to oak. If I could change my perception to the things in life that stressed and challenged me, if I could see them each as tools of temperance, then I could bear them all the easier. There would still be pain involved of course, but it would be pain with a purpose.

With this knowledge I was also more inclined to look for growth and to court adversity so as to quicken the growing, to get on the fast track. This is exactly what I did. The Latin adage for this is per ardua ad astra—through hardship to the stars. I put myself onto the front line and forced myself into situations that were just beyond me, sometimes completely beyond me, and then weathered the storm. And when my mind and body felt weak and I felt like throwing in the towel, I would remind myself that discomfort was my growth. When the critics went to work I saw them as sparring partners, I scrimmaged with the negative thoughts that tried to devour me. And one of the things—the biggest thing—that always carried me through was the fact that I had God in my corner, I had God all around me, and I had God inside me. I always knew that whatever should come about I had the Big Man backing me up. And he has never let me down. For those that don't follow a God and are at this moment recoiling like an offended thing by the mere mention of His name, for those that are their own god or for those that don't believe in anything outside this plane, use whatever it is that drives you for an internal support. I do believe in God, I love him but I don't insist that you or anyone else does, I respect everybody's right to follow whatever they like. If your God is a sacred mouse or a pint of beer, that's OK with me. I once asked Jimmy Boyle, the great international sculptor, whether he followed a god. He said no, he was his own god. He was the creator of his own truth. Who cares what name you put to it or even if you call it Blod (my wife sees God as an energy, something bigger than the name God itself. So when we go to bed at night instead of saying God bless, we say Blod Guess), call on it to help you temper a steely blade.

If I ever feel sensitive to criticism I always lay the facts on the table and tell myself (very positive self-instruction is vital for building an internal physique), that criticism is just an opinion, and everyone is entitled to theirs even if it is only to say that they hate my guts. It is not a glove across the chops or a challenge to 'fight at dawn, sir', it is an opinion, nothing more, nothing less. If you do not allow people their opinion without becoming aggressive, what does that make you? A bully. I don't want to be a bully, I want people to have their opinion even if they use it to slag me off. I'm

226

happy that I have the self-control not to worry about what others think of me. I'm happy with myself because I am an eagle and eagles do not feel threatened by flies. Neither would a lion hunt a mouse. I also remind myself that, more often than not, the person criticising doesn't really know me at all, and if he did he would probably feel very bad about what he is saying. I think about the person throwing the mud and I remind myself that they are flesh and blood the same as me. I humanise them. Very often we allow our critics to become monsters in our minds when really they are probably rather sad individuals with no life beyond their poison pens. If I want to have a laugh about the whole matter, I picture the critic scribbling away so fast and so angrily that smoke is firing out the top of their pen. I imagine how angry they are feeling because I don't answer their letters; I imagine steam coming off them because they have heard on the grapevine that 'Geoff Thompson forgives you'. If I want to feel compassion for them, to humanise them more, I imagine them with their wives and kids, with their mums and dads. I try to see them as much as possible as sentient beings. I always, no matter what, forgive them. I might cross them off my Christmas card list but I still forgive them. One particular gentleman (you know who you are and I forgive and love you), spent three years writing the most awful and abusive letters about me to a magazine. I can't tell you how upset it made my lovely mum. One of my friends rang me one day and said, 'Geoff, what are you going to do about it?'

I said, 'I'm going to forgive him.' That was it. End of story. Nothing more to say.

These people are the stormy weather that temper the oak; welcome them and don't protest when God sends you a weight-lifting set to build an internal physique.

The opposite of this, of course, is the fact that we hate it when the critics slam us but we tend to love it when they revere us. Someone once said that fame and failure were both impostors and that we shouldn't pay much heed to either. If you rely on other people's compliments to make you feel good then your life is going to be constantly up and down. You give your control to people when you rely on their acknowledgement. It is nice when you are appreciated, and if people tell me that my work is great I am flattered, and as I have grown in my work and my life I have often needed this exterior support to keep me going, but I don't hire the Ritz for a party when I get a good review. I love my work, I love me, I love being Geoff Thompson, I enjoy waking up and thinking, 'What does the day hold for me? What am I going to do today to grow?' It's enough to love your own work and hope that others get it and that in some small way it might serve humanity. So learn to disregard what others say, you do not need others to like your work or even to like you. You just have to learn to like the person in the mirror. That's enough.

Don't get off too much on great critique and you won't fall over dead when the inevitable bad critique lands on your doorstep.

And remember: the dog barks but the caravan moves on.

Epilogue

I hope you've enjoyed *The Elephant and the Twig* and that the fourteen rules for success and happiness have given you some insight into what kind of potential we all have, and how very exciting it is out there. More than anything I hope that it helps you to realise that you may be held back and it may feel like you are tied to a huge tree, but you're not, it is only a twig: snap it and be who you want to be, fill your CV until you have to hire a truck to carry it. Prove to those around you that you can do whatever it is that you set your heart on, prove it to yourself. More than anything, realise that you are your own god, this is your world as seen through your eyes and only by you. If you don't like it, change it, mould it, forge it, make it a heaven and do it now while time still allows.

God bless you.

Geoff Thompson
(on a beautiful rainy Saturday about to go and make a cup of tea and have a well-earned break) in a secret location somewhere in the Midlands.